The Limerick Homer

Tim Smith and Joe Green

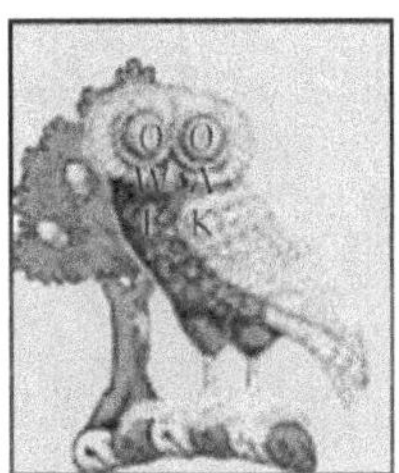

Owl Oak Press

Published by Owl Oak Press
101 Calle de Quien Sabe, Carmel Valley, CA 93924
USA

ISBN: 978-0-9770380-8-4

Manufactured in the United States of America.

First printing, 2008

Contents

U.S.A.
MISSILE
LAUNCHER

Introduction

Hello,

joegreen66@yahoo.com

smith@wheelwrightassoc.com

Dedication

To Connie, Johanna and Kris (Joe)

To the Irish Kidds and Smiths whose shades are lifting a pint in Hades. For my wife, who keeps me from joining them there.

The Limerick Iliad

Book One
The Tiff by the Ships

[The invocation to the Muse, A tale not for the ladies, The reckless toottootaling of Agamemnon, A priest scorned, Apollo on the beach with a bow, A charming diversion, An old fellow advises Achilles, Achilles, a melancholy warrior, The passions of Breisis, Augurs and Bulgars, Paris, the most beautiful man in the world, The taking of Breisis, A walk by the hoar sea, Mother to son, A nymph visits a god, Achilles quips as the Trojans attack, The banquet of the gods omitted]

Sing, Goddess, the wrath of Achilles
That gave all the poor Achaeans the willies
And sent many to Hades
Though some lovely ladies
Think it all quite boring and silly.

It all began with two guys
Who were both more willful than wise.
They fought over a dame
I can't remember her name
It ended in "eis" I surmise.

The poor girl was taken in war
By King Agamemnon…this happened before
The events in my verse
So I'll be quite terse
In truth it's all quite a bore.

Agamemnon was macho and brutal
And thought she was part of his loot. "I'll
Keep her with me

By the sweet wine dark sea
And dilly and dally and tootle."

But her Daddy thought he was a beast
And her Daddy was Apollo's priest
And told the dumb King
She was none of his bling
And insisted that she be released.

But Agamemnon just laughed at her Dad
And said "She's all mine...too damn bad!"
And stroked her patootie
And called her his cutie
Which made her father quite sad.

So her father implored his dear God
"Oh, help me! Oh holy A-Rod!
And smite those damn Greeks,
Those perverts and freaks."
And Apollo gave him the nod.

He got his bow and sat on the beach
And for his invisible arrows did reach
And shot the Greeks down
With their mules and their hounds
Then rested and nibbled a peach.

And Achilles sat sipping some wine
Until just about Day Number 9
When Patroclus said
"Hey, have you noticed the dead?"
Achilles said "No, but you're looking fine!"

Achilles was, per usual, lushed
And Patroclus didn't want to be rushed.
Achilles said "Come here you charmer
And help me take off my armor."
And what happened next is hush hushed.

Odysseus peered through a rent
in the side of Achilles' tent.
He drew back with a start
and clutched at his heart
crying, "Zeus, I hope they repent!"

For Patroclus, young and unscarred
but lithe and supple and hard,
had dropped to his knees
and grabbed Achilles
by his root and made him see stars.

And Odysseus was acting ridiculous
All in all he was quite TravisBickleous
All Love is sweet
And the Greeks found all Love meet
Although it is often doomy and fickleous.

All over, all passion spent
Achilles still hung around in his tent:
"To Hell with this crisis.
Go and bring me my Breisis!"
And Patroclus, obedient, went.

Breisis came in and submitted
Though she thought Achilles dim witted
She thought Achilles a heel
With no sex appeal
And to sweet amour quite unfitted.

And we know that the reason's because
Achilles loved dear Patroclus
But he made the motion
As if he needed a Trojan
Denying the kind of a guy that he was.

Achilles, though possessed of great bulk,
Had a sad inclination to sulk
So he let his feelings fester

When that busybody Old Nestor
Burst into his tent and said "Let's talk!"

Dropping poor Breisis and wheeling
Achilles cried "Yes, I've lost touch with my feelings.
But I have nothing to say
So please go away
And to hell with your sexual healing!"

But Nestor persisted anon:
Saying "Brave Achilles, don't fawn
And weep for this boy
Who gives you such joy
There's a battle beginning at dawn."

And Nestor kept on repeating
"Hey, you better go to the meeting
King A has gone crazy
You better be there in case he
Insists on us taking a beating.

For that asshole's pissed off Apollo
Put your armor on, no time to wallow.
I heard the king say
At the end of the day...
I'm going there now. C'mon and follow!"

And both of those cads turned their backs
On Breisis who thought them sad sacks
And when they had gone
That fine lass got it on
With both the greater and lesser Ajax.

But poor Breisis herself she did censor
And God knows the true faith portends her
Repentant sob session
And her true confession
To a priest named Ajax the Cleanser.

Up on Olympus lounged honey-thighed Hera
With Zeus on his golden chair… a
Right buxom goddess
Who loosened her bodice
And said "Sweetheart, you don't seem to care-a.

You know that I favor the Grecians
For all sorts of whimsical reasons
I should think you would frown
Apollo is cutting them down
While you entreat my lascivious pleasings."

Zeus sighed and offered her nectar.
Said "You know I'm for the Trojan sector.
Have you seen Helen of Troy?
I have and oh boy!
Besides, I rather like that young fellow -- Hector.

Now come back here dear honey-thighed Hera
There's no need yet to despair, ah.
After all I am Zeus
And you know it's no use
To deny me you never could dare, ah."

Ah, the heavens thundered and sputtered
Until Hera was thoroughly futtered.
Then Zeus had a snooze
And Hera hit the booze
And cursed at the fellow and muttered.

Down below King Agamemnon the Vulgar
Listened to Calchis the wisest of augurs.
Who said "Listen to me.
Set your prisoner free
Stop acting like a hairy ass Bulgar."

They also called King Agamemnon "The Fair"
Although he had lost almost all of his hair
And looked like Telly Savalas

But if you live in a palace
There's nothing else the dear people would dare.

Achilles was quite a fair youth.
Ok, I'm not quite telling the truth
In a way he was handsome
But he seemed like Charles Manson
When he stabbed you and shouted "Forsooth!"

The most striking fellow was Paris
He looked stunning in armor or bare-assed
And was named after a city
Which seems quite a pity
For somehow it made him embarrassed.

And while the Greeks were ranting and raging
Helen found him extremely engaging
All the sweet girls loved silly him
And not just in Ilium
They all loved both his person and staging.

Ah, but let us return to the Achaeans
Who felt just then so achey-breakyan.
It's a lot to endure:
A nine year old war
With leaders so stupidly adamantean.

King Agamemnon finally said "Oh, ok
I guess you mofos want it that way.
I'll end the crises
But I'm taking Breisis!
If I have to send the other away!"

The Achilles walked by the hoar sea
And wept and cried "Why me, oh why me?"
Then told his pal
To go get the gal
And give her to that damn bourgeoisie.

Then the youth made a despairing motion
And cried out aloud to the ocean.
His mother Thetis appeared
Man, it was quite weird
She began rubbing him down with some lotion.

"Oh, Mother," he sighed "How I wish
That I was, like you, a half fish
And lived in the dark
And drank Cutty Sark
And acted in ways very kitsch.

But you went and made me a hero:
Though the net result will be zero,
And I'm doomed to die
And I don't even know why
I feel queer, like a painting by Miró"

Thetis cried "Oh, never my dear!
I'm in touch with a guy: Edward Lear.
And in an immortal poem
You'll have your home.
Fame and Glory forever! Don't fear!

He's invented a verse form immortal.
I saw it through Father Time's portal.
You'll get back at that prick
With a great limerick!"
Which didn't cause poor Achilles to chortle.

"No, mother, I want glory and riches
And to get back at those sons of bitches.
Ask Father Zeus
Or else it's no use.
And it must occur with no hitches!"

So Thetis went up to Olympus
Oh, how those damn gods always pimp us.
Zeus said, "Oh, that's cool.

I'll let the Trojans rule.
Though for the Greeks my dear wife quite a simp is."

Achilles returned to his ships
With his sharp swords hung by his hips
And the Greeks cried "Alack"
At the Trojan attack.
And Achilles just smiled and made quips.

So endeth Book 1 by old Homer.
Rendered by moi. Hi, howdy, I'm Gomer
And if you get dyspeptic
If I call this an epic.
I admit that it's quite a misnomer.

**Book Two
Agamemnon's 115th Dream and the Catalogue of
Ships**

**[An apology to the reader, Homer's method
questioned, The Dream Diary of a King, Tricked by
Zeus again, A King tests the mettle of his subjects,
The King's subjects haul ass outta there, Ulysses
scapegoats the tribes of Israel, A few Jews killed,
Everyone feels better, The actual catalogue of the
ships and who was in each and how so and so begat so
and so omitted for the busy reader]**

Though the Iliad on the whole is alluring
I'm afraid that Book Two is quite boring.
A catalog of the ships
And some geography tips
Is enough to wreck your own ship in its mooring.

So Old Zeus came up with a scheme:
He would send that vile King a false dream.

Which is rather odd.
After all, he's a god.
And you would think his power supreme.

But the dream came upon old Aggie while sleeping
And said "Enough of your worries and weeping.
I got it from Zeus
That you are Il Duce
And your victory will be rather sweeping!"

Then Old Aggie awoke quite excited
And the fellow was still quite benighted
For he thought it best
To try out a test
Which could render most of his hopes somewhat
blighted.

He summoned all to a great general meeting
Then sadly offered this greeting.
"It shall come to pass
That they'll kick our ass."
And that didn't need any repeating!

As soon as he said the last word
The Generals said "By the Gods have you heard
The Trojans are comin'?
You can hear their drumin'!
To stay on this beach is absurd!"

Then word spread to all of the men
From Ms. Amanpour from CNN,
Who got out of there fast.
She, however, was passed
By a preacher crying "Amen."

Brave Achilles was quite disgusted.
It seemed that all of his dreams had been busted.
The Greeks ran about on the sand.
Each one quite unmanned.

And there wasn't a damn one he trusted.

But, look, why its Ulysses in the midden!
Shouting "Damn it, the King was just kiddin'
It shall come to pass
That we'll kick THEIR Ass.
If you thought he meant something else, why he didn't."

The Greeks cried "By Zeus, that's great news."
And blamed everything on those goddamn Jews.
And grabbed a few peddlers
Yes, wicked Jew meddlers
And burnt them. Then became quite enthused!

As Ulysses went through the host
knocking their heads with his post
He said, "Don't be shirkers
what we need are berserkers
who'll turn Ilium into toast!"

So they all hurried back to their meeting
to find out where all this was leading.
But Thersites was pissed.
Agamemnon he dissed
'till Ulysses gave him a beating.

Then spoke brave Ulysses to all
"I know you'd all like me to call
down a host of fine virgins
to assuage all your urges
but, damnit, first scale that wall!"

But the Argives were ready to leave
and they raised a great shout by the sea.
Nestor stood and he shamed them
Agamemnon then tamed them
and on victory they all agreed.

Then Athena urged them all to battle

and to stop all the pussified prattle.
"Get out there you Greeks
and slaughter those geeks.
Off your asses and into the saddle!"

Now comes that moment you're dreading.
I admit that it could be rough sledding:
A catalog of the ships
And their significant trips
And an account of Penelope's wedding.

So...this is the end of Book Two.
We are kindly deferring to you:
"Readers Digest Condensed"
Because we have sensed
You have something much better to do.

Book Three

Ménage a Troy

**[The armies move together, The character of Paris
questioned, Paris volunteers to fight Menelaus in
single combat, They fight, Aphrodite spirits the most
beautiful man in the world away, "We'll always have
Paris," A Ménage a Troy]**

Ah, the two armies so quickly did gather
But they didn't start fighting, they'd rather
Watch a cool duel
Between those two fools
And engage in the usual blather.

Ah, Fate! You're a damnable dealer:
A war started by a lying wife-stealer!
I can't help but feeling

This would all be more appealing
If it were written by Garrison Keillor.

Ok, the plot is beginning to thicken.
And Paris, of course, is a chicken.
But if you're lot is
To be loved by a goddess
You know that you're heart will keep tickin'.

So Menelaus just almost spears Paris
Which would leave a certain goddess sans his caress
So she spirits the boy
Back to Helen of Troy
Exclaiming "We'll always have Paris!"

Paris says "Thanks Aphrodite!
And Helen slips into her nightie
And visits celestial places
In the young Trojan's embraces
And cries out "Oh, Paris, the Mighty!"

Book Four
The Armies Clash

[From Here to Eternity, To Hell and Back, So it goes]

Ah, but this is no tale of amour.
It's an epic of another damn war.
So, all Hell was let loose
With the end of the truce
Which I neglected to mention before.

Menelaus got hit by an arrow
And was ready to go to his barrow
Until he saw at last
The arrow never got past
His armor. His escape was that narrow.

The battle began in grim earnest.
Before long many would need an internist
And many be dead.
What else can be said?
Hecatomb and Fiery Furnace.

Which caused a little concern in the Heavens.
At this time I believe there were seven.
"Zeus can you spare a
Moment?" said Hera.
And the lightning flashed in the levin.

The Gods huddled up on their hill
And, at times, disagreement was shrill.
The Goddesses claimed
That it was all just a game
And that only the bad would be killed.

Zeus called on his daughter to go
And stir up some shit down below.
She flew through the ranks
Turning all the Greek cranks
And winding them up for the show.

So together the armies did clash
with the Greeks, early on, kicking ass.
The Trojans were whipped
until Apollo quipped
"Horse tamers, charge them, and fast!"

And many a noble man fell
and their souls ferried over to hell.
Darkness fell on their eyes;
Their corpses drew flies;
And for neither side it went well.

Homer starts naming the dead.
"But what's exactly the point?" Vonnegut said.

I simply propose
To write "So it goes"
Have a few drinks and then go to bed."

**Book Five
The Fighting Sullivans**

**[Theo-Feminine Anger, Diomedes, inspired and
guided by lovely Athena, smites assorted Trojans ,
"Diomedes kills Pandarus" omitted in deference to
the Swan of Avon, Is he mad? Attacks a goddess, The
God of War condescends and is wounded, Ares
speaks bluntly of his hurt feelings and returns to
Olympus]**

One Greek had eaten his Wheaties
His name I recall: Diomedes;
And there were many poor boys
From the city of Troy
Who would never return to their sweeties.

Diomedes was especially mean: a
Bully inspired by Athena.
Homer speaks of his glory.
Well that's not my story.
I can't think him exactly divina.

He rolled through the Trojans like fire
leaving bodies to burn on the pyres.
He got shot in the arm
but it brought him no harm
for Athena was moving the wires.

She constantly guided his spear
and filled Trojan hearts with great fear.

Diomedes went mad
and he really jumped bad
when lithe Aphrodite drew near.

He stabbed with his spear at the goddess
and pulled at her delicate bodice.
Divine fluids flowed.
She fled from his hold.
but dropped her poor baby, Aeneas.

Then things really got hairy
and she cried for her brother, Ares.
"Go kick that Greeks butt
he called me a slut.
Zeus! This war thing really is scary."

Then the gods get involved in the fray
and the killing goes on night and day.
Ares gets stabbed,
but is fixed by his dad.
And is now safely out of the way.

Book Six
A Battle, A Leopard-Skin Pillbox Hat, A Tender
Scene, Hector and Andromache

[Homer strokes his zither, Menelaus captures
Adrestus, but Agamemnon hath no mercy unto him,
Diomedes shows he is a gentleman, An affecting
domestic scene, Queen Hecuba distresses Athena,
Hector's wife's name proved unpronounceable, I
always thought Bellerophon was a horse, Helenus
gives advice to Hector, Paris arrives invigorated by
his amours]

The fight on the plain went on thither
And then, by the Gods, went on hither

While on an isle far away
On that lovely Spring day
Homer sat stroking his zither.

First Ajax killed the best of the Thracians
Then all one hundred and one of the Dalmatians
Who went down to dog hell
And shattered Hell's bell
With their howling against those damn Grecians.

Euryalus killed Dresus and Opheltius
And then killed Aesepus and Pedasus
Who were the twins sons of a naiad
And this saddened a Dryad
Who cried "Those Greeks are such blasphemous
badasses!!"

Menelaus chased Andrestus in his chariot
While singing and waving his lariat
And Andrestus fell on his tush
On a Tamarisk bush
And soon checked into the Infernal Marriot.

He got to his feet. He was living!
Then begged on his knees for forgiving
And promised a ransom
A ransom quite handsome:
Gold that never stops giving.

And Menelaus nobly assented
But his nasty old brother prevented.
Ag said "Kill them all.
The great and the small."
So Menelaus nobly relented.

The Trojans fell back and fell back
But the Argives stopped their attack
To grab weapons and gold
From the young and old

And fine armor straight from the rack.

"You fools!" cried out Nestor the Sage
"Don't you know this is the Bronze Age?
Let's sack that damn city
Sans ruth and sans pity
And put Ezra Pound in a cage!"

To Hector, Helenus said
"You must fight, or else we're all dead.
Make a stand here and now,
I'll go slaughter a cow
And hope that Athena sees red."

Hector defects to his Mom.
Tells her what's going on,
"You must go to Athena
And offer the Queen
Something that you have on."

The Queen frowns from where she sat
As Hector points at that!
Although she consented
I don't think she meant it:
"Not my leopard-skin pillbox hat!"

When Hector is gone the queen goes
For her bangles and ribbon and bows
And selects a chapeaux
She don't want no mo
And to Athena's temple tiptoes.

"Dear Goddess I give this to you
Please let all of us please just pull through.
Here's my favorite hat.
I hope you know that
We'd appreciate all you can do."

Hector talks to his mother,

Sees Helen and his brother.
He calls Paris a punk.
Helen sits in a funk
and says, "I'm a bitch like no other."

Hector visits his wife.
Says "Yo, you're the love of my life.
But I am a man
So you must unnerstan'
That I follow the zither and fife.

"Besides you know it's all fated.
We stand here already dated."
Then he kissed his sweet child
And his dear wife went wild.
And the Fates quite terribly berated.

Hector's helmet gleams like the sun
as his brother comes up on the run
Says, "Sorry I'm late"
Hector says, "How I hate
that, of you, all my warriors make fun."

But one day we'll sort this out,
that is, if the Grecians we rout.
But it's all up to Zeus
So we better hang loose.'
And for Book VI that's over and out.

Book Seven
Highway 61 Revisited

**[Hector and Paris leave Troy, Rejoin the fighting,
Athena does not accept Hecuba's sacrifice and wants
a leopard-skin pillbox hat, Athena and Apollo plot,
Take it all down to Highway 61, Hector vs. Ajax no**

**decision, An interlude for the dead, Paris "I will not
give back Helen. We're in love!"**

Hector runs out, shouts "Let's roll!"
Which might seem quite good for the soul.
But Paris snapped back,
"Hey, this isn't Iraq
And you ain't no Texan asshole.

Then the Trojans were kicking Greek ass.
So two gods met in some pass.
The one from the Greeks
Was the first one to speak
And it was Pallas Athena, alas.

"I want all those damn Trojans to die!
You seemed shocked. Well, you want to know why?
I'm telling you flat
It's because of the hat
It was her second-best one!" she did cry.

"Yes, to you that would logically follow,"
Lisped the pride of the Trojans, Apollo,
"But if you adjusted it right
And in a certain light
You could look somewhat like an older Frieda Kahlo.

But Apollo of the Hyacinth Curls
Was always a guy for the girls.
"Ain't it just like a woman
To mix all this doom in
With their fog, their amphetamine and their pearls?"

So the gods hatched a plan that was chillin'.
And taking a cue from Bob Dylan:
That each side should send one
Man out on Highway 61.
Hector, for the Trojans, was willin'.

But the Greeks were quite taken aback
and of courage, they suffered a lack
Till shamed into action
they at last got some traction,
rolled the dice, and out popped Ajax.

Ajax said, "Man I'm ready to rumble
please pray that I don't take a tumble."
He then marched up to Hector
like Hannibal Lector
saying, "You ready? Come on man, don't mumble!"

Hector led with a spear that deflected,
Ajax countered and hit Hector's neck. (ed)
They both fought like heroes
but Hector scored zeros.
the gods called it a draw, what the heck. (ed)

They parted with honor and graces
returning to respective places.
Each side celebrated,
bodies were cremated,
but pale fear shone in all of their faces.

For Zeus plotted bad things for them,
although oxen were roasted for him.
That son of a bitch
really had a bad itch
to fuck with these fellows called men.

And Hector returned back to Troy
And was greeted with ambiguous joy
And Ajax went back
To the Grecian barracks
To dine with the Greek hoi polloi.

And Nestor had too many martinis
And in a scene by Fredrico Fellini

Cried "Let's bury our dead.
And then go to bed."
The questionable moonlight shone greenly

And the corpses glowed quite phosphorescent.
On the whole it was awfully unpleasant
As they gathered them up
While still in their cups
And burned them till they were quite deliquescent.

And the Trojans burned up their own corpses
And Hector the Tamer of Horses
Suggested that Helen
And her magnificent melons
Be returned. A plan that every Trojan endorses.

The Paris stood up and was pissed
And said "Nay, never! On this I insist.
I'm keeping her here.
But, never fear
Just send someone down to the ships.

And tell those Greeks sons of a bitches
That I'll gladly give up all their riches
That I took away
On that lovely day
From those fine-haired sons of a bitches.

If that ain't enough kindly add
That they also may take that fine lad
Yes! Ganymede!
Who will meet every need
That they won't even know that they had."

Now, this may seems to you a good deal.
But this ain't like our ancient Greeks feel:
They cried out "He's nuts.
No ifs ands or butts!"
And so Paris lost his appeal.

And so we leave the Greeks fearfully grinning:
Scared, though they insist they are winning.
You'll never get rich
By digging a ditch. (Which they did)
They hoped it was the top of the inning.

Book Eight
The Gods Must Be Crazy

**Homer gets dissed for his epithets, Zeus bullies his
buddies and sides with USC, Diomedes and Nestor
show some hair, Hera and Athena rip Zeus a new
one, Zeus shakes it loose.]**

Homer writes of "Dawn's rosy fingers."
One applauds how the image does linger.
But like most men
Homer says it again and again
And seems dreadfully proud of his zinger.

Now it is time for a "Homeric epithet."
I used to know why but now I forget.
They begin with "Just as"
And include "All That Jazz"
And are the height of poetic etiquette.

Up on Olympus the gods are assembled.
You don't want to know what this resembled:
A George Bush cabinet meeting.
Zeus promised a beating.
And the gods all simpered and trembled.

So Zeus, that prick, (what a bully)
shows the gods that he's in charge fully.
He thunders and bellows,
"If you fuck with those fellows

below, I'll kick your ass duly.

Yes, Zeus went all crazy and wild.
I'll beat you all like a red headed step-child."
When the gods were all cowed
Only then he allowed
That he actually felt quite serene and quite mild.

Athena then said to him, "Dad,
I knew we've all acted bad.
But it would be nice
if we could just give advice
for the killing goes on and it's sad."

Zeus said "My Omnipotent Mind
Would actually like me to be kind."
Took his chariot to Ida
An there did abide
A-looking for what he could find.

Yes, Zeus went down for a gander
at the war by the river Scamander.
On his scales he would weigh
who would win on that day.
Oh how bloody the Ilium sands were!

He looked at the slayees and slayers
And their children saying their prayers
Put his thumb on Fate's scales
Ignored their cries and their wails
So much for the power of prayers.

Zeus sent down his furious lightning.
This time it was the Greeks he was frightening.
The Greeks started to run.
It just isn't done
To stand up against theological fighting.

All the Greeks started running but Nestor

But the old man was no God-Contestor
He just had a lame horse
And so, yes, of course
He'd soon be a hell-bound old quester.

The old fellow was a spirited old elf
But the Greeks cry "Every man for himself."
He was left there for Hector
Without a protector
To be stripped of his life and his pelf.

But Diomides cried out to Ulysses,
"Let's go help the old guy! Are we sissies?"
But Ulysses the Brave
His own ass did save
For he had to go home to the Missus.

Diomedes, to Nestor's aid came
and got him some help with the reins
They charged at old Hector
but his spear went off vector
And then Zeus started the rain.

And they ran at Hector full speed
Old Nestor and young Diomedes
And they killed Hector's driver
Leaving Hector alive
Or this story would be over indeed.

Diomedes advanced on the prince
But didn't get close to him since
That megalomaniac Zeus
Let some lightening loose
Which caused even drunken old Nestor to wince.

The Nestor insisted they leave
Which required young Diomedes to grieve.
"They'll think I was afraid!"
But Nestor just brayed.

"Damn it, I'll tell them what to believe."

Diomedes did not want to quit
after Hector had called him a shit.
But he knew that the gods
had stacked all the odds
and he didn't like it one bit.

Nestor whipped Diomede's ponies
Hector cried "You goddamn phonies!"
And remained comfortably seated
As they retreated
And shouted "You phony baloneys!"

Then Hector cried to Xanthas and Lampus
Who were horses. The poor guy's hippocampus
Looked like a bruised mango.
Hector hollered "Let's tango.
O'er the field and the plain and the pampas."

Fair Hera was watching all this
And she turned to Poseidon to hiss:
"Let's go help our guys!
What are you: the Lord of the Flies?"
A charge which Poseidon dismissed.

Hera said "To the devil with you, sir."
She inspired a cowardly archer named Teucer:
Who was a little creep
Who from behind Ajax would peep.
What's an old sea god to do, sir?

Teucer had been an ignominious bastard:
A cad and a creep and a dastard.
But, divinely inspired,
Every arrow he fired
Killed -- even though he was plastered.

First he killed god-like Lycophantes

And then Sergeant Preston of the Mounties
Who had become lost
And paid the ultimate cost
For pursuing Yukon Jack for the bounties.

But Hector he never managed to strike
So Ag said "Hey,what's there to like?"
The bad man kept on trying.
Lithe-limbed lads kept on dying
Boringly -- they all seem so alike.

Then Teucer killed Hector's driver Archptolemus
Who bellowed like a sodomized Hippopotamus
Which was nothing new, sir
To that little creep, Teucer
Who was a beastly beast of a beast sodomist.

The Hector tried a sneaky new tactic.
Please allow me to be a bit antiphrastic:
He got Teucer stoned.
I'm hoping you don't
Think this quite anticlimactic.

The Greeks ran through the trenches and stakes
And Zeus the forsaken, forsakes
While cow-eyed old Hera
Vamps like Theda Bara
Insisting on a few more damn takes.

Athena cries "How our father forgets
How I helped Hercules when he had the sweats
In Deep Tenebris
Fetching Cerebrus
From where the sun neither rises nor sets."

Hera said to Athena "Let's ride!"
And I guess you could say that they tried.
Zeus sent Delta Dawn
To say "You better not be gettin' it on."

So they stayed up in Heaven and sighed.

Then Zeus to Olympus returned.
Of course the great god was burned:
Said to Athena and Hera
"You see I don't care.
A fact one hopes you have discerned."

Then mean old Zeus got his licks in
Said, "Hera you're an impossible vixen."
But they all knew he was a mad
Hypocrite and a cad
Who resembled Richard M Nixon.

Then, of a sudden, Night falls.
Darkness the Trojans appalls.
They build great fires
And sit playing their lyres
And, perhaps, dream of masquerade balls.

Book 9
Going Nowhere Fast

**[Greeks get the willies, It's no go Achilles,
Agamemnon says go/Diomedes says no, Nestor says
whoa, Thetis gets a grip, Greeks seek to speak,
Achilles nixes Nestor's fixes.]**

You don't need a classical treatise
To know who to blame. Yes, it's Thetis
Who blubbered, said "Please!"
Embraced the All Father's knees
As she plied him with strawberry margaritas.

Some Greeks ran to Achilles' tent
And begged him, please, to relent.
He said it's high time.

You stop drinking my wine
And it's time that you go. So they went.

**Book 10
The Lost Patrol**

**[A brief literary diversion, Menelaus and
Agamemnon pow-wow, wardrobic descriptions,
Diomedes and Ulysses get sneaky but so do the
Trojans, Dolan is a dumbass, Two sneaky Greeks kill
the Thracians then go home to party**

and/or

**An egregious epithet, Agamemnon's enjoys some time
on the beach, Cool and refreshing after a long hot
day, Favorite cocktails of the Greeks, Nestor suggests
someone spy out the Trojan position, Diomedes
volunteers but asks for a second man, Diomedes
selects Odysseus to go with him, Hector calls for a
volunteer to spy out the Achaean ships, promises
Achilles' horses and chariot to sad ass Dolon the sad
ass fool, Dolon volunteers and sets off, Odysseus and
Diomedes interrogate Dolon then kill him, Odysseus
and Diomedes kill a bunch of Thracians as they are
sleeping, A piteous scene presented as sound military
policy, an allusion to Bob Dylan.]**

For years it seemed hard to tell
That Ulysses should be roasting in Hell
Then in "Troilus and Cressida"
Ulysses confessed to a
Nature quite shifty and fell.

He was the Greek's Great Persuader:
A smarmy and selfish orator
But his "honest word"

28

Was just as absurd
As a chastity vow from a satyr.

Just as Zeus will send lightning and thunder
To warn of war or some other wonder
So the Grecian king sighs.
Yet the question abides
Isn't this simile some sort of blunder?

Well, not if you're Homer the Greek
And applause from the noble you seek
You kiss their ass
And it shall come to pass
You'll dine in palaces wetting your beak.

Hence Homer's inordinate passion
For the particulars of aristocratic fashion
For the nobility care
"Tell us, what did he wear?
I understand Agamemnon was really quite dashing!"

Agamemnon donned the skin of a lion
To cheer him up, to help with his sighing
And he had "comely feet"
And sandals quite neat
Which cheered up the Greeks who were dying.

He sauntered off to chat with his bro
Who wore the skin of a panther you know:
A goodly array
That he bought from E-bay
Guaranteed to frighten the foe.

Agamemnon said "Bro, I'm so nervous.
Looks like Zeus has done us a disservice.
And I feel quite let down
By all these guys just laying around
I'm not sure that these cowards deserve us."

And Menelaus replied to his bro.
"Those poor guys are dead, don't you know
Looks like we are screwed
But somehow I feel imbued
To just go along with the flow."

Ag said, "Stop smoking that weed.
Gimme some. I know what we need.
We need some brave scouts
To go poking about
So listen and follow my lead."

With this he gestured to Nestor
"Get up, dear old fellow, and pester
The Kings of the Camps
To come to me bearing lamps
If you see Breisis, damn it, arrest her."

Now the king and his brother admit
that their greed got them into this shit.
With the gods taking sides
they're afraid for their hides
and Diomedes thinks them both twits.

But Nestor, of course, has a plan
says, "Diomedes go find a man,
a tough son of a bitch,
for you two'll cross that ditch
and try to force old Hector's hand."

Then comes wardrobic descriptions
and we're told that Odysseus looked bitchen'
in his crafty hide hat
with boar's teeth and all that,
he was smarter than Christopher Hitchins.

They both prayed that they would prevail
and continue this tedious tale
which, ad infinitum

lists every damn item
and, against which, Proust's work is pale.

Across the way Hector was tricking dumb Dolan
Who certainly wasn't a Solon
His father was rich
But the poor son of a bitch
Only had trophies for bowling.

Hector suggested that he be a scout
And the plans of the Greeks go find out.
And Dolan agreed
But said he would need
Achilles horses -- without any doubt.

Hector agreed to the plan.
To give the divine steeds to the man
But the prince, yes, of course sees
That Achilles' fine horsies
Can only belong to one man.

And that man, is, of course Achilles.
They are, after all, divine fillies.
And if another man tried
To take them for a ride
He would very soon be pushing up lilies.

Then Dolan donned the skin of a wolf
He thought it made him look somewhat aloof.
And, grin and bear it,
He put on the skin of a ferret
And thought that made him look tough.

This is all an ironic contrast
Of the sort Homer thought would long last.
He thought it quite clever.
But, boy, should he ever
Subscribe to Writer's Digest, and fast.

Dolan tripped on a rat who was nibbling
On a poor wounded Trojan who was quibbling
With his only friend, Death,
To come and take his last breath
But Death was busy taking his sibling.

Dolan was caught and he started crying.
Ulysses laughed, "Have no fear of dying
We'll hold you for ransom
A ransom quite handsome!"
But wily Ulysses was lying.

And Dolan told them all that he knew
And all that he didn't know too.
Then Diomedes said,
Grabbing him by the head,
"Too bad. It's all up with you."

Then Dolan babbled "No, please."
Diomedes cut off his head with some ease.
And his head still was talking
As his poor ghost was walking
To Hell's ferry to give Charon his fees.

This was years before the Geneva Convention
A fact I feel we should mention.
They once were taught
But it's a long time since we ought
To be quibbling about moral pretensions.

So the gods once again were implored
to show the Greeks where, with their swords,
they could whack out some Thracians
as they slept at their stations,
and they went about it with no words.

Till Apollo woke old Hippocoon,
but, alas, it was not soon
enough to stop the slaying,

he saw his men decaying,
and the horses gone, all left in ruin.

So the two: Diomedes, Ulysses
killed a dozen and stole all the horses.
Hustled back to the ships,
collected their tips,
washed up and got drunk with their forces.

Only the dead now are sleeping
And the red dawn once more is peeping.
So we won't go on
About where the flowers have gone.
Now ain't the time for your weeping.

Book Eleven
Enantiodromia

**[Greco-Roman confusions, Zeus switches sides, that
prick, then switches back! Hector heats up, Diomedes
kicks ass, gets shot in foot, Nestor advise Patroclus,
Achilles and Patroclus dally, A mid-point
interjection]**

and/or

**[An anachronistic invocation, Ulysses' real name
revealed as Ermes Effron Borgnino O'Sisyphus,
Many Greeks with names ending in "us" and "er"
killed by Agamemnon, Paris wounds Diomedes in the
heel, Patroclus dreams a love that cannot be named
while playing with a platypus, Nestor's dumb plan]**

Christ on a crutch on a bike.
Homer overuses that word "godlike."
Of course, the gods were such jerks
It ironically works

Gods and men that way so alike.

And you'll notice we call Odysseus "Ulysses"
And sometimes we call Ulysses "Odysseus"
They're both AKA's
For a single ofay
Whose real name was Ermes Effron Borgnino O'
Sisyphus.

Zeus, for no particular reason,
Decided it would be the Achaean's' season.
Ok, half a day.
But what can you say?
When you're a god, none dare call it treason.

So he sends down Strife, that damn whore,
to incite the Greek hearts more to war,
Agamemnon gets dressed
in his bright Sunday best,
accessorized by a jaunty gold sword.

And Homer describes the guy's shield
Panic and Terror out in some field:
The same macho madness
The same gangsta badness
That long ago should have been sealed.

But we remain vicious and dumb
Witness, for example, the Somme
And all of the asses
Laddies and lasses
Who hanker for the Kingdom Come.

And then Agamemnon shouted
While the gods up in Olympus pouted.
They were quite put out
That Zeus intended a rout
They were quite Argive besotted.

But it was a splendid fine morning
For the Greeks who had little warning
That a bit after noon
They would be almost ruined.
They should have been mourning that morning.

Agamemnon slew Oileus, and Bienor
While humming a medley from "The Entertainer."
He then killed Isus
And then he killed Antiphus
Who were the sons either of Priam or Prince Ranier.

Then he captured Hippolochus and Pisander
There by the river Scamander:
Sons of Antimachus
Chips off the old blockus
Which raised Agamemnon's royal dander.

So Agamemnon up and then slew them.
Their greedy old daddy had screwed them.
He cut off their heads.
I think that's what Homer said.
Their heads rolled and the Argives all booed them.

Agamemnon charged like a insane fierce lion.
All the Trojans ran from him flying
Like a bunch of scared cows
With a lion tearing their bowels.
The simile's Homer's. You buying?

But Zeus had something in store:
yet another turn in this war.
He filled Hector with hope
saying, "Don't be a dope,
just wait until Aggie gets sore."

Just then Aggie was wounded by Coon
but it didn't yet cause him to swoon.
He kept the top billing

and went on with the killing
but trouble was coming, and soon.

Hector saw Agamemnon in trouble
and knew that Zeus had burst his bubble.
With a mighty war cry
he screamed, "Let's get that guy."
And took off over the rubble.

Yes, Hector feels as good as before
He thinks this a splendid war
And kills many a man
The Greeks do what they can
But there's a sale on Greeks in Death's discount store.

And now Hector went on a tear
and the Greeks were left tearing their hair.
For great Zeus had decided
with the Trojans he sided,
yet Diomedes and Odysseus were there.

The two noble Greeks make a stand
and many men die by their hand.
Diomedes gets hit
by Paris, that shit,
While Odysseus does all that he can.

Diomedes strikes Hector's Helm.
And shouts "Dog, you're no peer of the realm!"
As Hector takes off
With a headache and bad cough
And a penchant for Bollywood film.

Diomedes is now in a tizzy.
But isn't that Paris? Oh, is he
Bending his bow?
Well, yes, well you know
He's taking him out. Viz. he

Is Shooting Diomedes in the foot with an arrow
Fletched with the tail feathers of a sparrow.
It goes though his foot
And he seems to take root
As the arrow pierces his marrow.

Diomedes finds this effete:
A real man doesn't shoot another man's feet.
But Paris just laughs
And signs autographs.
The Trojans think this quite neat.

Like jackals and beasts in the hills
the Trojans close in for the kill.
But Odysseus holds them back
until helped by Ajax
and escapes because of his skill.

And so the killing goes on
And Zeus gazes down while crying "Tres Bon!"
As Ulysses is faced
With getting out of that place.
And it looks like the Greek hopes are gone.

On the beach that young fellow Patroclus
Was playing with a duck-billed platypus.
He built a sand castle
Away from the hassle
Of war and its impertinent blunderbuss.

But he dreamt of Castor and Pollux
And of their brotherly frolics.
If he could show Achilles,
That they could be like these
He'd have him, at last, by the ballocks.

He expressed this to Nestor who said
"By God they'll all be struck dead.
If they don't know it's you!

Here's what you do.
Go put on his armor!" he said.

Patroclus said "I'll have to ask his permission
But I know how to help his decision."
He put some rouge on his lips
And then ran to the ships
And stepped aboard with no little frisson.

And Achilles still hangs by the sea
with Patroclus athwart his broad knee.
He says, Pat, go find Nestor
and make a request or
tell them all to come supplicate me.

Well now that we're half the way there
you, dear Reader may ask, "But who cares?
We reply from our hearts
that the limerick arts
are too precious for us not to share.

**Book Twelve
A Bridge Too Far**

**[Martian tourists before Troy, the disgusting
Venusians, Polydamus has a plan, The Warrior Code]**

We are now in media res.
Thank the gods that Homer never wrote plays.
One would be wishin'
For intermission
And not thinking of laurels or bays.

We've neglected to mention the Martians.
Mene mene tekel upharsin.
They were there with their saucers
Having responded to offers

And having neglected elementary precautions.

They had signed up for an expensive Jazz tour
And expected to be at the Apollo stage door
To see John Coltrane
Walk out "After the Rain"
And not be at no damn Trojan war.

They gave their computer the "Apollo" command, ah.
How could they know they would land, ah
There on a plain
With the macho insane
Instead of with Coltrane "Live at Birdland?" Ah!

And then there were the Venusians.
Who were in Troy disguised as Rosicrucians.
They were there to steal Helen
And worship her melons
And titter and make vile ablutions.

All of this old Homer leaves out.
He'd rather describe the brawl and the rout.
Mention "Polydamus."
You sometimes need Camus
To figure out what it is all about.

He would say the whole thing's existential
And point to its lack of potential
And agree with old Sartre
That the whole thing lacks art
And is not, on the whole, consequential.

So Polydamus makes a suggestion
To Hector, "Sir, there is no question.
That crossing that ditch
Will be a son of a bitch
And lead to clinical depression.

I suggest that we charge on our feet

That way we cannot be beat."
So the Trojans did.
Too bad for that kid.
It led to a horrible defeat.

The defeat was a long time in coming.
The Trojans seemed quite alarming.
But our narrative fails
And we'll spare you the details.
We think that would be rather charming.

And Sarpedon speaks of the warrior code, oh
In a quite out of the fashion old mode, oh.
He says, " Since we're the patricians
It's part of our mission
To take on the heaviest load, oh!"

But that's not the way of our ruling class:
Who give all the rough stuff a pass:
Like Cheney and Bush
Who sit on their tush
And let others go under the grass.

It all ends as the Achaeans retreat
And the Trojans kill the elite:
Tenny or twenty.
There are so many
A songbird goes tweety tweet tweet.

Gird your loins for more of the same:
both sides fighting with might and with main.
But, unlike Iraq,
when you get to the back
the ending will be very plain.

Book Thirteen
The Trojans Break Through.

Greek sheiks tested.

**[A brief commercial announcement, Sea and Sky, A
close shave for Aeneas, Paris wigs out, A bloody good
ending]**

and/or

**[A word from our sponsor, If you don't know what
"Pelegian" means, look it up, Hey, Pancho, Hey,
Cisco!, Paris prefers cigarettes for Frenchies, The
slaughter continues]**

Oh, yes, in case I forget
Book XIII is brought to you by Kent cigarettes.
When you sulk in your tent
Go ahead! Smoke a Kent!
And you'll wonder where your yellow has went!

Zeus turned his eyes from that fatal shore.
He thought it just might be a bore
And he looked upon Kali
At a charity rally.
And thought of his Lost Lenore.

Neptune was the brother of Zeus
And had almost all of his juice.
He was feeling Pelegian
Under the Aegean
And was getting prepared to bust loose.

He thought he'd set the Greeks a fine sample
Of what it's like to be an example.
Talked to those pathetic sad sacks
Greater and lesser Ajax
Until their manhoods began to be ample.

Idomeneus was the Cretan honcho
And was Cisco to Meriones' Pancho
"Hey, Pancho, Hey, Cisco!
This is brought to you by Nabisco
Shredded Wheat makes a fine lunch-o!"

Oh, I see who I think I see is
That lucky old fellow Aeneas
Who on all of his raids
Shaved with Gillette Blue Blades
And thought "If only Old Dido could see us"

And Paris looks like a dream
With his hair slicked back with Brylcreme!
Yes he is a man's man.
He's smoking Gitanes:
And for after the battle -- Jim Beam!

Coming up next, don't miss Car Talk!
And a posthumous interview with Bela Bartok.
This unmoved mover
Is going on maneuvers
Rather tired of this BS and war talk.

But enough with these silly-assed ads
for the Greeks things look pretty bad.
Ajax calls Hector out
Hector says with a shout,
"I'll ensure that your ending is sad."

The sea and the sky god are brothers.
Its clear that they hate one another.
Poseidon and Zeus
won't broker a truce,
Please, someone call Rhea, their mother.

Poseidon, the Achaeans supports.
Zeus likes the Trojan cohorts.
So the killing goes on

and ensanguines each dawn.
Oh, how the gods love blood sports!

Book Fourteen
Gods get Horny Too.

**[Nestor wakes up and smells the carnage, Hollywood
comes calling, A brief outing in NYC. Zeus and Hera
do the dirty boogie. Ajax rocks the Trojans' world]**

and/or

**[Agamemnon at the cabana with Nestor, The
marvelous bazongas of Helen of Troy, Why We Fight,
Divine erotica, Hera and Brando, Gods, Sprites,
Fairies, Unicorns were popular once, Hera's ascent
into Never Never Land, The Marvelous Love Making
of the Gods, Forsooth, Zeus seduced, Zeus in
Dreamland, The Achaeans strike back, Difference
between Achaean and Argive not explained]**

Nestor was hearing-impaired
So he didn't know how the battle had fared.
He was in his tent
Where he had been sent
And from the awful truth had been spared.

He went out with his bronze-clad spear
And muttered "Oh, dear. Oh, dear."
The Greeks were flying pell mell
They weren't doing so well
And he started to break down like King Lear.

Just as a wave in the ocean
Waits with no particular motion
This way or that
Old Nestor sat

Like an elderly hung over bosun.

Should he go assist on his side?
Or go find the King? Has he died?
So he turned away from the fight
Not feeling quite right
"This is all so confusing," he sighed.

And there, voila, was the great King!
With the noble wounded all in a ring
Under a big beach umbrella.
What splendid fellows!
They listened to the mermaids sing.

The good fellows were on R&R.
A nearby cabana had a fine bar.
Mixed drinks were half price
Though there was a problem with ice
Which is the price that must be paid in a war.

Nestor ran to them, cried, "My God! A Disaster!"
And they drank faster and faster.
"Well that's too bad."
Said the King, "I'm quite sad."
Of understatement he was deemed a master.

"Well, boys, looks like the party is over.
Let's set sail for the White Cliffs of Dover.
We'll met again
Don't know where. Don't know when.
And we'll be rolling in clover!"

This made old Nestor quite skittish.
"No long good byes now! We're British!"
Agamemnon was mad!
And that was too bad.
"Oy veh!" Ulysses cried out in Yiddish.

"Have you forgotten the melons of Helen?

Ah, they could turn a saint into a felon
We'll stay here as long as
Those marvelous bazongas
Are not ours! How long there's no telling."

And with this he sent up a shout
And King Neptune, that sexist lout
Sent up a roar
That almost blew in the door
Of Heaven where Hera did pout.

She looked at Zeus bored on Mount Ida
And thought "By God, I can't abide a
Self satisfied creep
If only I could put him to sleep."
And into her secret room she did glide-a.

She looked a bit like Marilyn Monroe
And in that secret room don't you know
In a special place
She kept a photograph with the face
Of her true beloved: Marlon Brando

Oh, how that guy could send her.
He was so attentive and tender.
Marlon longed for the divine
And they'd drink honeyed wine
" I could'a been a contender."

She gave his sweet image tender looks
Then got out her sexology books.
She would seduce
That horrible old Zeus
And she took down her gowns from their hooks.

With ambrosia she removed any soil
From her body then applied olive oil
Specially scented.
Oh, how she resented

Zeus. "That bastard could use a moyel."

She put on a marvelous gown
Then encircled her blond hair around
With sweet golden braids
And a scuncie of her maid's
To keep one delicate wisp down.

Then to Aphrodite she flew
Said, "I need to get that girdle from you.
I need it for my Mom
My mom and dad ain't getting it on."
The Love goddess's curiosity grew.

"You mean the girdle of love and desire
And of sweet flattery entire?
To lend to your Mom
So she can be a love bomb?"
Aphrodite knew she was a liar.

Aphrodite wished she could discover
Who exactly was Hera's secret lover.
But she gave her the girdle with a smile
Thinking all the while
"I wonder who's lighting her fire?

Then up up and away Hera did hurry
To the land of the Sandman and the Tooth Fairy.
The Easter Bunny
Thought she looked quite funny.
But he's just a bunny. Why worry?

When there old Hera had the habit
Of having tea with the Mad Queen and the White Rabbit
Then she would jaunt off to Never Never Land
With Tinkerbell and Peter Pan
Then go to Alabama to a concert with Black Sabbath.

She was met by some dwarves and Snow White

Whom she informed of her plight
So she went with Dopey and Sneezy
And Dom DeLouise
To Sandman's Palace of Perpetual Night.

Which was a Jazz Club up in Harlem.
And the Sandman said "Ok, Darling"
You just play this Soft Jazz
After all that pizzazz
And old Zeus will nod off to New Orleans."

Should we describe how Zeus was beguiled?
How Hera played Good Girl Gone Wild?
How Zeus fell into slumber
After Hera's Rockette number
And curled up and snoozed as he smiled.

Well, we will if you visit our website
www.oldmanzeusgoodnight
And register there
For our Internet Fair
To learn how to improve your lovelight.

We have the best uncut video
Showing what Hera to Zeus exactly did-e-o.
The footage is raw.
You'll see what they saw
As they did and they did and they did-e-o.

But while the immortals were screwing
strange things down on earth started brewing.
Sleep said to Poseidon
"Zeus is out like a light, mon!
His crack at the sack he'll be rueing."

And the combatants heard all the commotion
made by Poseidon great god of the Oceans.
He led Greeks with his sword
and the wild battle roared

like the sea in perpetual motion.

But Hector was showing no fear
and when bold Ajax drew near.
Although Hector looked glorious,
his arm was notorious
for missing the mark with a spear.

Then Ajax hurled a huge rock
that spun Hector about like a top.
It knocked him out on his ass
but his friends showed up fast
so the story line won't have to stop.

Hector's loss to the battle was costly
and the carnage ensuing was ghastly.
There were eyeballs popped out,
wounds from gizzard to snout,
and the tide of war turned pretty fastly.

For Ajax was foaming and mad,
he went on a one-man jihad.
Favored by all the gods
he beat all the odds
he's as tough as an old Brillo pad.

**Book Fifteen
Yo-Yo Mama**

**[Post-coital blues, Trouble in Paradise, That '60's
Show, Poseidon takes a dive, Hector revectors, Ajax
sternly defends]**

and/or

**[Please hold your tongue and say "My father works in
a shipyard," Quetzalcoatl brings chocolate and**

**basketball to the Trojans, The Great God awakes and
is pissed, The vomitus of Hector, Tamer of Horses,
The odd adolescence of Poseidon, Poseidon revealed
as co-author of Billy Budd, More fighting and death]**

The tide, as it were, once again
is turned by the gods on poor men,
who'd like to quit fighting
but gods keep inciting
them on. Will it end? Who knows when?

If you've wearied of death,
I advise you, don't hold your breath.
Yet we know that a limerick
is quite the best trick
for conveying both passion and depth.

Perhaps this is all anecdotal
But once the god Quetzalcoatl
Went sailing past Argos
With many strange cargoes
This was back when the gods were more motile.

He gave the Trojans tobacco and chocolates
And he liked to walk around the block a lot
Smoking a Kent
And raising the rent
And chatting about the apocalypse.

But Quetzalcoatl had to go back-o
No more chocolates and tobacco.
He had a sixth sense
That he better go whence
Before the Trojans got the old sack-o

Do you know why a Trojan is a condom?
Because when the Greeks made the breach then they
Sommed them

Killed everyone
And when they were done
It was if the Enola Gay had done bombed them.

Hector was vomiting blood
Ajax shouted "I'm in the hood!"
And when Zeus saw all this
Man, he was pissed
And he didn't act as nice as he should.

"Do you remember when I strung you up high?
Right up there in the sky?
And bound up your hands
In unbreakable bands
And pounded you with banana cream pies?

It can happen again vile deceiver!"
Hera protested. He didn't believe her.
He said "You're a witch
And a cunning old bitch
Why can't you be more like June Cleaver?"

For Zeus loved sixties TV
And it wasn't that easy to see.
For you are all alone
Without "The Twilight Zone"
When you're stuck way out in BC.

Hera flew swifter than thought
In that beautiful gown she had bought
Told the gods what she knew
But what could they do?
Before they act they already are caught.

Hera said, "Oh, Ares, your poor son
The valiant Askalaphor is undone."
Ares shouts, "Now, I'll go
To Troy down below
If Zeus wants a fight then he has one!"

And he called for Panic and Terror
But Athena said "Que sera sera."
And reminded him that
Zeus would knock his ass flat
And Ares allowed that he'd spoken in error.

Hera panted to Apollo and Iris
"Zeus has commanded, 'Come to Ida and admire us.'
Yes, he used the royal "We."
So they flew over the sea.
In such a hurry Apollo didn't know where his lyre was.

Zeus was resting in a scented pink cloud.
Iris and Apollo curtsied and bowed.
"Iris, go to Poseidon
And sit down beside him
And tell him this shit is no longer allowed.

For I first came out of the womb
Of Rhea in that primordial gloom
And if he wishes
To sleep with the fishes
That will be his inevitable doom.

One morning he'll wake up in bed
With his favorite seahorse's head
And he'll end up just bones
Sleeping with Davy Jones."
That's what the God Father said.

Poseidon was the "Encircler of the Earth"
And he said to Iris "What's that worth?
We are brothers three
So, he's older than me?
Mom always thought of me firth."

Yes, Poseidon had an unfortunate lisp
And sometimes spoke like old Quentin Crisp

But of Quentin Crisp's wit
He had not a bit
Not a touch, not a shred, not a wisp.

He was to be the future sea god.
As a boy he was very odd.
He had a speech impediment.
Liked to play in the sediment.
And had seaweed all over his bod.

He felt, at a loss, without purpose
And he was examined by a medical porpoise
Who found him autistic
Hence quite unrealistic
With an unfortunate case of herpes.

One day Zeus kicked sand in his face-o
Poseidon said "Get offa my case-o!"
But here's what Zeus did.
He got a big squid
And rubbed it all over his face-o.

Then Poseidon's face turned quite squamous:
Scaly, and squishy and charmless.
And he got depressed
And thought it was best
To stay up in his room in his pajamas.

And he would hardly ever go out
He stayed up in his room and did pout
And became very odd
Doubting the existence of God
And wondering what it all was about.

Poseidon went back under the flood.
Between Zeus and him there was so much bad blood.
He still wanted glory
So he started writing a story
With Herman Melville called "Billy Budd."

The story contained all that he missed
A beautiful boy -- fated, death kissed.
And down in the sediment
He agreed with the sentiment
"I am sleepy and the oozy weeds about me twist."

Zeus had his way with Poseidon
then called Apollo to his side and
told him to go down
to that dark killing ground
showing Hector whose side he was on.

He found Hector with stars in his eyes
and said, "Man, I'll tell you no lies,
Almighty Zeus
has cut Poseidon loose.
It's gonna be a good day for you guys."

So Hector became a mad dog
with his whip, men and horses he flogged
screaming, "Lets go, you Trojans!
We've got Zeus' mojo and
for us today, victory is progged!"

The Greeks were pushed back to their boats
across all of their walls and their moats.
Then that charmer Patroclus
said, "I'd better go help us."
leaving Eurypylus with his goats.

And thus ends this part of the tale
with both sides locked in a stale
mate of killing.
If Achilles were willing,
we know the Greeks wouldn't fail.

Book Sixteen
The Naked and the Dead

**[Patroclus implore the melancholy Achilles to send
him back to the war to help the Achaeans, Paris hides
behind the arras with the help of Special OP Harris
and overhears how Achilles may be killed, Paris at
Woodstock, Tra la la, Patroclus sallies forth, Bites the
dust.]**

Dear Readers, soon you will learn
how the gods' will Fate's wheel may turn
grinding life from each man,
spreading blood over sand,
such that, for atheism, he'll yearn.

Oh, we live in degenerate days
That once might not have been true, anyways
Once there were nymphs
And you could catch a glimpse
Of angels and fairies and fays.

This often made life more endurable
But in Homer it made life more deplorable
i.e. the Greek Gods
Here Homer nods
They seem completely mad and incurable.

And who can guess what's really in store
as Patroclus himself goes to war?
Achilles may pray
but it won't save the day.
Ah, foreshadowing is such a bore.

Now Patroclus, to Achilles comes crying,
"Alas, all our buddies are dying!
I've just seen the light,
I must join in this fight,
I hope you don't think that I'm lying."

Achilles then calls him a wuss
and says his own anger is just.
But that he never meant
just to hang in his tent.
It's over now, what's all the fuss?

He looks with love at his charmer,
and offers to loan him his armor.
Says, "Lead my Myrmidons,
and go after those huns!"
Then took the fair lad in his arms.

But, of course, they weren't the only ones there
As they fooled about there in the chair.
For there was Paris
Hiding behind the arras
And a passle of the sprites of the air.

There were the spirits from the "Rape of the Lock"
Were they there only to mock?
What else can I see?
A lonely banshee
And "Wachet Auf" by Johann Sebastian Bach.

Paris hid behind the arras and tittered.
The sprites sailed through the air. How they glittered!
And the lonely banshee
And, yes, the Fiddler of Dee
Looked on and seemed somewhat embittered.

On the whole they found it fantastical
That this ridiculous scene should be "classical.:
"Sleepers Awake"
That scene did forsake
For the scene seemed somewhat bombastical.

How did Paris get behind that old arras?
He employed a special op name of Harris

Their secret headquarters
Was under the waters
Between deadly Scylla and Charybdis.

But while these two Acheans dallied
Hector toward Grecian ships sallied.
Zeus was pimping Ajax
by breaking his ax
while the Trojans set fire to his galley.

Achilles wore size 50 armor.
Patroclus was a size 42 charmer:
So his armor was padded
With billet doux cladded
With some old paperbacks of Philip Jose Farmer.

Patroclus went into the battle well-greaved
And all of the Trojan deceived.
Armor covered his back
Unlike the poor guys in Iraq:
A horror hard to believe.

Achilles shouts to the gathered Myrmidions
"Boys make your hearts as obsidian!
And sensitive readers
Are not Yes Indeeders
They'd rather be reading Joan Didion.

Then Achilles goes back to their quarters.
The Martians fire up their transporters.
He makes a secret sign
And gets some rhubarb wine
Which he purchased at a Phoenician importers.

He takes just one judicious sip
Then removes the cup from his lip
Pours the wine out
So Zeus wouldn't doubt
That he is, on cue, as per script.

He offers up a longwinded prayer
To the God of the sky and the air
For his friend's return
But soon he would learn
That the God Father just wasn't there.

He recites again his sad story:
How he was born bound for glory,
How it seems unreal
That a wound in his heel
Will turn him into Greek Cacciatore.

His rough hands in prayer he clasps.
Groans and can't hear Paris' gasps.
Paris catches a ride
With a Martian named Clyde
That fatal knowledge the equivalent of an asp.

But sadly that Martian was stoned
And his translator module intoned
"Ok, let's rock!
We're off to Woodstock!
I'm one ET who doesn't want to phone home."

What could Paris do? There was no stopping him.
That Martian was stoned and looked like a goblin.
So Paris grooved with the hippies
And tripped with the trippies
And had a passionate ten minutes with Janis Joplin.

At this point I should explain relativity.
But I won't. I lack the proclivity.
But Space and Time
Are like gin and lime
Hence the cosmic nativity.

And, to continue, the gist is
Explained by Hermes Trismegistus

Everything is eternal
And a God could discern all
The possibilities and all of the vistas.

And all that is all will occur
In Space Time where there's no "as it were"
Which is much more mysterious
And deeply delirious
Than all our God Notions concur.

Consider the immensity of space
And how we are stuck in this place
This makes joke of all
Our notions local
Insisting we have seen God's face.

No, I won't explain my explanation
But it's a source of endless fascination
It will be in the prequel
Or maybe the sequel
And will cause a major sensation.

Patroclus cries "No more touchies and feelies!"
Gets in chariot and does a few fine wheelies.
The Myrmidions shout
As they sally out
The Trojans see and feel a bit queasy.

Yes, Patroclus enters the fray
and things start to go the Greek way.
Men of Troy get the willies
for they think he's Achilles,
the bravest of all men, and gay!

Is that Achilles?" they say
"Nah, can't be, really no way!"
But see how they run
Cry "We are undone!"
When Patroclus puts a dozen away!

He leads the Daanans to glory
slaughtering all in his path, very gory.
Hector tries to hang tough
but enough is enough,
he knows Zeus is changing the story.

Patroclus and his man Meriones,
who both had enormous cojones,
attacked all the Lycians
who turned and were fleeing
then Apollo yelled, "Pat, go back, homey!"

But Patroclus was too damn proud
and he kept charging into the crowd.
The gods grew annoyed
at this arrogant boy
whose hubris would soon be his shroud.

Wounded and chumped by the gods
Patroclus faced terrible odds.
Had he heeded Apollo
better days might have followed,
and the Fates to him made a nod.

But none of these things were to pass
for this day was Patroclus' last.
Hector stabbed at his belly,
his knees turned to jelly,
and uttered these words at the last:

"Hector, you got sloppy thirds.
Boast on, but you'll eat your words.
You're not a god, you're a man
and your death's close at hand."
Then his soul fluttered off like a bird's.

But Hector cried bullshit and said,
"How do you know I'll be dead?

When I meet Thetis' son
I may be the one
in the end, that comes out ahead."

Now the stage is finally set.
But we're not to the ending, just yet.
For our croupier, Homer
told me, "Listen up, Gomer
red or black pal, place your bets.

**Book Seventeen
Patroclusgrad**

**[Trojans and Greeks fight over the body of Patroclus,
This book perfect of its kind don't change a thing,
Paris opens in Vegas, Paris appreciates Italian
cinema and larger metaphysical implications
suggested, Bob Dylan again]**

They fight over Patroclus's body-o
But Patroclus don't care and drinks a rum toddy-o
On a houseboat on the Styx
With John Wayne and Tom Mix
Awaiting the arrival of his buddy-o.

Homer's Iliad is thought to be sacred
But it actually is quite inaccurate.
The reasons because
Paris was
At Radio City with Burt Bacharach.

While his brother fights over the stiff
Paris gets over his lisp
Knocks Vegas flat
With "What's New Pussycat"
And helps Hendrix out with a riff.

Zeus spreads a battlefield fog
Paris sees "Andalusian Dog."
And makes it his project
To advance dream logic.
A Trojan's cut down. Bleeds like a hog.

Dying, the men become symbols.
The bridge at midnight trembles.
They go into the silence
Of no ideals and no violence.
"The country doctor rambles."

Book Eighteen
The Arms of Achilles

**[Auden's great poem, Do look up "hippocampi, The
Shield of Achilles, Achilles and Tarzan of the Jungle]**

From "The Shield of Achilles"

"A ragged urchin, aimless and alone,
Loitered about that vacancy; a bird
Flew up to safety from his well-aimed stone:
That girls are raped, that two boys knife a third,
Were axioms to him, who'd never heard
Of any world where promises were kept,
Or one could weep because another wept.

The thin-lipped armorer,
Hephaestos, hobbled away,
Thetis of the shining breasts
Cried out in dismay
At what the god had wrought
To please her son, the strong
Iron-hearted man-slaying Achilles
Who would not live long."

Achilles would have felt he was gipped
If he got THAT shield from Hephaestus thin-lipped
The Genealogy of Morals
Goes down in swirls
That, inevitably, lead to the crypt.

And he had God on his side.
And also his best friend had died.
It's a significant thought:
What has God wrought?
"And the rushes cried Abide! Abide!"

All these myths want us to forget
Ho! to battle! Hurrah! Well met!
Patroclus's real last words
Which were the usual absurds
Of "Oh, no! Not me! Not yet!"

Brave Achilles is on his ship's prow.
Antilochus arrives and now:
"Your friend is dead."
Is really all that he said
And all Achilles could do was howl.

From the sea came a myriad of Nereids
Except two who were having their periods
A poet named Doris
And a transgendered mermaid named Morris
Who didn't think the whole thing was too serious.

Leading them was Achilles mom, Thetis
With Doto and Proto and two lovely Ritas
Saw Achilles there
Tearing his hair
"My boy, is this a nice way to greet us?"

They had arrived on fantastic hippocampi

Except for a Goth Chick riding a lamprey
With her green hair in a bunchy
Bound up by a scunci.
The other Nereids thought she looked tramply.

And Achilles begins to recover
(As I read this passage over and over).
Mourns for his friend
And his untimely end.
But continually mentions his armor.

The Greeks had a "Culture of Shame"
So what "Achilles" is is a name
Always the hero
Consequently my dear
He can screw up again and again.

The Greeks look and say "Godlike Hero"
He's our guy and without peer-o!
So he is mad
And nasty and bad
"He is ours! Out wonderful hero!"

And in the Moronic Inferno
Where we presently twist and burn-o
Our president
Is a heroic gent.
Talk about the Eternal Return-o

But, by the gods, how strangely declined
Our Fate seems to be signed.
If we had just puts Fats Waller
On the greenback dollar
We might have escaped from this bind.

Achilles vows eternal vengeance.
Thetis can't promise transcendence.
Paris says "Gotta go"
Finding disco

Without any doubt quite horrendous.

Thetis says she'll go visit Hephaestos
The goddess Iris Achilles' guest is.
"Get up and fight!
"You know this ain't right!"
Oh, god how these gods do test us!

"They are fighting over the corpse of your friend
And it's almost over. The End.
The Prince of Troy
Is dragging away your boy.
This can't be. Heaven forfend!"

And Achilles replied that he couldn't
And it wasn't because he just wouldn't.
He had no chain mail.
And so would inevitably fail.
His death would be pointless and sudden.

But Iris, that importuning bitch,
Said, "Ok, just go out to the ditch."
And pinked him up in a cloud.
And made his voice loud.
The overall effect was appallingly kitsch.

He stood on the ditch and he bellowed
So that the Trojans who thought he had mellowed
Ran for their lives
And fell on their knives
Their brave spirits shaken and yellowed.

They knew they were all gonna die
Because it sounded like Tarzan's cry!
They were looking for Cheetah
As they beat a retreat a
Gleam of fear in all of their eyes!

Then Hera the Ox-Eyed Queen

(Called that by Homer the Mean)
Sees them on the run
And pulls down the sun
Then joins a cruise to the Caribbean.

She' so upset that she's shakin.'
It's a cruise she should have already have taken.
She smokes great ganja
Yodels like Mario Lanza
In the arms of a juked up Jamaican.

The Trojans know some shit is coming
but they sit about hemming and humming
about how many may die
feeding birds from the sky
as the jackals and hounds come a running.

Hector don't like what he hears
he thinks Polydamas full of fears.
He says, "Jesus H. Christ,
what are you all? Mice?"
Of course then, they broke out in cheers.

Back at their ships, all the Greeks
mourned Patroclus with tears on their cheeks.
Achilles felt bad
for Patroclus' dad
who he'd promised a share of the treats.

Achilles rages. Exclaims. "This is it!
I'll find twelve Trojan children whose throats I"ll slit
Then put them in the fire
Of Patroclus's pyre."
Which would have appalled even that pirate, Jean
Laffite.

Then they cleaned poor Patroclus' corpse
with hot water and oil, of course.
He was wrapped up in wool

(which, this season, is cool,)
and the Myrmidons wailed as a chorus.

Thetis went crying to Hephaestus,
"At making armor, you are the best!
My son's lost his armor and friend
in this war without end.
Can you fashion some bronze for his chest?"

First came his work on the shield:
a work of universal appeal
Recreating a story
of the world and its glory.
He hammered, and forged and annealed.

Then, on the armor, he got busy
working hammer and tongs in a tizzy.
Helmet, sword and some greaves
were quite the bee's knees
and he cranked them all out in a jiffy.

When finished, he brought them to Thetis,
and laid them ablaze at her feets.
Thetis said "Thanks Hephaestus,
though you limp just like Festus,
your workmanship just can't be beat."

Book Nineteen
Force One from Skyros

**[Pajocks and pantaloons, Look up Pentimento and
appreciate the elegant effect, Achilles mopes, More
moping, A Talking Horse, Apollo in a Disco in Frisco]**

This is Book Nineteen, of course.

The tension builds with a bewildering force.
It begins with an apology
And ends in a doxology
Pronounced by a talking horse.

Thetis brings the armor to her son
Who exclaims, "Look what the good gods have done!"
A strange sentimento
Since there's no pentimento.
Achilles fate already spun.

Then Achilles worries about flies:
How they could be eating his dead friend's eyes.
Thetis says not.
The poor boy won't rot.
Honey and nectar corruption defies.

Then Agamemnon says "I'll give back Breisis.
I admit I'm no good in a crisis
It was the goddess Ate
And a bad latte
And the conjunction of Ares with Pisces."

And Achilles said "All right. That's fine.
But let's go. Let's kill that swine."
And Ulysses defers
But says he prefers
A brief rest and some divine sign.

They eat but Achilles abstains.
They talk of ancient campaigns.
And Ulysses the wonk
Their consciousness zonks
By discoursing on John Maynard Keynes.

Zeus turns and says to Athena
"Go and make like Sabrina
Feed Achilles honey and nectar
So he can kill Hector

And be a proper killing machina."

So now Achilles is prepared.
Who knew how much the gods cared?
And, of course,
He spoke to his horse
While the trumpets and bugles blared.

His horse's name was Xanthos.
And they stood by the river Scamandros.
"You soon won't be alive
But this time you'll survive."
Neighed Xanthos who felt quite misandros.

Then Achilles cried "Ok, right let's go!"
While Paris was hating disco.
Thinking he might go home
He took out a comb
In the restroom of a gay bar in Frisco.

He also knew Achilles must die.
He didn't know how it all worked or why
But as he looked in the mirror
Behind him appeared ...
"At your service. I'm Marty McFly."

Book Twenty
Von Achilles Express

**[Zeus tells the gods to go down and fight, Hera back
from her cruise, Aeneas to fight Achilles but he has to
live to be in the "Aeneid" so is spirited away, Gods
fight, then sulk]**

Cronos' son then launched relentless war.
He told the gods to go to the killing floor.

"Choose up your sides
My love always abides
Disregard how I was acting before."

And the gods gave a rousing great shout!
And flew down from heaven's redoubt.
They had been bored
But now they adored
This chance for an immortal freak out.

Hera had returned from her trip
And went to the assembled ships.
She had returned with a tan
And a retirement plan
For placing Trojans in various crypts.

With her came Poseidon and Hermes
Who wanted Troy to go to the wormies
And Pallas Athena
That prima ballerina
And Hephaestus with his significant infirmities.

But long-haired Phoebus, archer Artemis ,and Xanthus
Flew downward to the Troyan campus.
And they also had Ares
And a few renegade tooth fairies
And Aphrodite holding her lampus.

Apollo says "Aint we got fun?"
To Aeneas: "Man, you are the one!"
Aeneas said "I gotta go home
Then go sailing, found Rome
So sorry Son of the Sun."

Apollo says "But your mom's Aphrodite!
Why do you take that so lightly?
She's a daughter of Zeus
And her power let loose
Will overcome the old man of the sea, quite rightly.

Achilles' mom's just a silly sea naiad
Similar to a sprite or a dryad
And her Dad's just Poseidon
While your mom's dad's Mr. Lightning!"
"Ok, I'll go" Aeneas sighed.

Hera, hearing this, gets quite upset
and wants to double the bet.
But Poseidon says chill
and avers that they will
do better not to enter just yet

The gods flew to get the best views.
Zeus stayed in Heaven amused.
Although the fix was in,
They shook the welkin
Cheering and calling for brews.

In these days when wars have gone global
We forget the strange rites of the noble.
Before they begin fighting
Aeneas must enlighten
Everyone that he's upwardly mobile.

But first Achilles must insist he get back
And go get a publicity flack.
If he wants fair fame
And an immortal name
This is the wrong plan of attack.

Then Achilles reminds him of when
Aeneas lounged by his old cattle pen:
Achilles came up with his spear
And just by the force of his sneer
Made him light out for the territory like Huck Finn.

Aeneas said, "So your mom's Thetis.
I was Aphrodite's first fetus."

Then he talked about horses
having strange intercourses
with the North Wind, whoever he is.

Aeneas than recites the necrology
Of his noble and divine genealogy
And again mentions, of course,
That marvelous horse
An absolute freak of biology.

"The North Wind was that noble steeds sire!
And he grazed in my ancestor's shire!"
Then he threw his spear
"Let the heaven's give ear!
The rain is Tess, the fire's Joe and they call the wind
Mariah!"

Aeneas and Achilles square off!
But Poseidon avers, with a cough.
"I'm feeling all hollow
for that bastard Apollo
made Aeneas think he was tough."

He knows that Achilles will win
so he heads down in the din
and rescues the Trojan
with his powers mojoan,
but Achilles thinks it a sin.

Hector and Achilles then rally
their troops urging them not to dally.
Then, they come face to face
but it's not time, nor the place
for the battle royale's sad finale.

For the gods, once again, take a hand,
intervening down there on the sand.
Apollo and Athena
reset the scene-a

though the hatred still burns in each man.

So each one goes off his own way
and each finds so many to slay.
Limbs are hacked, guts are spilled
spines are splintered, many killed.
In all, it's a horrible day.

Book Twenty-One
Achilles Fights the River

**[Remember the scene at the end of the Godfather?
Baptism -- then cut to this or that hood being offed?
We do that here. Rather well, Achilles attacks the
Trojans hiding in the river Xanthus (also called
Scamander), takes twelve young men alive to sacrifice
for Patroclus, Rolling in the river, What
Schopenhauer would say, Who was the mother of
Helen?, Did Zeus really have sexual congress with a
swan, Could it have been a goose?, Trojans race for
the gates!]**

Achilles was never a giver
Yet even the gods in their immortal flivvers
Godding about
Gave an incredulous shout
When he began attacking a river.

The Trojans had fled to its banks
Then ran into the water, their ranks
Shattered and broken.
"Heaven, Hell or Hoboken!"
Shouted the gods clapping hands, giving thanks.

Achilles jumped into the stream.
Paris listened to "A Love Supreme."

He was listening to Monk
Getting quietly drunk
While Marty McFly laid down his scheme.

Achilles thrust with his sword.
Monk hit a diminished chord.
And the river ran red
As McFly said
"We better be getting aboard."

Paris said "Wait, let me hear "Ruby My Dear-o"
None of this is exactly too clear-o."
But Marty leaned back
And put on the Eight Track
And slapped the DeLorean into first gear-o.

Achilles slaughtered thirty men-o
He grew a bit tired so then-o
He took twelve Trojans boys
To be his toys
He'd slit their throats at his friend's funeral when-o

He suddenly saw young Lycaon
Whom he had captured and enslaved long time gone.
Achilles had assumed
That the lad had been doomed
But here he was living anon.

He suspected some theological plot
But was unconcerned. He was not
Going to show mercy
And so, somewhat tersely.
He informed the young fellow he'd rot.

The unarmed boy grabbed the slaughterer's knees
And screamed and cried "Oh, please, oh please!"
Achilles said "I wish
To make you food for the fish."
And gutted him and threw him into the river with ease.

The Greek warrior was on a mad tear,
who he killed, he just didn't care.
He met Asteropaeus
son of the river Axius
and sliced him in half like a pear.

Then comes a horrible section
where cold eels come from every direction
to feast on his guts
while fish nibble his nuts.
Leaving no hope for his resurrection.

The river Scamander cried out
to Achilles, "Damn it, cut it out!"
He then called to Apollo,
Saying, "Man, why won't you follow
Zeus' plan? Put an end to this rout!"

Then the river got pissed and attacked,
knocking Achilles right on his back.
He thought he would drown,
for no gods were around.
His composure was starting to crack.

Now the gods start to rage at each other:
even immortal sister and brother
go for each other's throats.
To Zeus it's a joke,
knowing that Hera's their mother.

Athena knocks Ares around
then takes Aphrodite right down.
Saying, "Don't be a silly one
it's curtains for Ilium."
Aphrodite did not make a sound.

Poseidon then challenged Apollo.
Apollo replied "It don't follow

That we divinities
Containing infinities
Should fight over these mortal fellows."

Artemis shouted "You cringing poltroon
You'd run away from the man in the moon!"
Apollo hissed
Said "You skanky bitch"
And the dish ran away with the spoon.

Then Hera caught the goddesses' hands
Ignoring her unpleasant demands
Then took her bow and her quiver
And then did deliver
A slap that knocked her down to the sands.

She got up and flew to her Pap.
And wept and wriggled in the Olympian's lap.
One could conclude...
But that might be too rude
Was Zeus ever brought up on that rap?

Here's a chance for an Homeric excursus
As the Trojans bring out the hearses.
This fellow so strict
Was a sexual addict
To list his lovers would take hundreds of verses.

In the beginning old Zeus loved Metis
As she tended her garden picking lettuce
She tried to avoid him
Which only annoyed him.
What an example he set us.

The next thing he did? Well, he ate her.
Swallowed her like an alligator.
The sad reason was
Well, just because
He was Zeus and a vile Pantocrator.

The poor goddess was heavy with child.
In the bowels of Zeus she was really damn riled.
Athena was inside her
But she was a fighter
And emerged from the forehead of Zeus in a while.

Which you would think he'd find rather unpleasant.
But he hardly noticed. He wasn't
Too damn sober
So he only rolled over
And continued schlepping some peasant.

And we could go right down the list
Of everyone Zeus more than kissed.
But you'd be annoyed.
Go read Hesiod.
He even screwed the Goddess Nemesis!

Some say she was the mother of Helen
Some say that was Leda. There's no telling.
As Schopenhauer
Explains with some power
in Die Welt als Wille und Vorstellung.

On one side we have the poet Yeats
Though many scholars claimed he screwed up his dates.
Perhaps Zeus came as a swan
And exclaimed "Tres Bon!"
But right now Priam shouts "Open the gates!"

The Trojans were panicked and ran
To escape from that horrible man.
Priam wept
As Helen slept
And dreamt of a triumph at Cannes.

The Greeks get quite close to the city
and this makes Apollo feel shitty.

He sends godlike Agenor,
out the front door
but knows that he'll die. What a pity.

So in front of the great city walls
to man-killing Achilles he calls,
"Dude, go back home
and just leave us alone
for you know that we Trojans have balls."

He tosses his spear at the Greek.
His aim is good, but his arm it was weak.
Then Peleus' son
Takes out his gun
And attacks the poor Trojan geek.

But we know Apollo is lurking
and soon enough, his magic he's working.
He saves Agenor's hide,
stands by Achilles' side
loops his cunning chain and starts jerking.

Achilles thinks Apollo's Agenor
And runs after him and it's just before
They arrive at the Scamander
That Apollo with candor
Says Agenor's been taken away heretofore.

And so the book ends with a chase
and the Trojans all trying to race
back through Ilium's gates
to avoid their sad fates.
Destruction's a hard thing to face.

**Book Twenty-Two
The Death of Hector**

**[The Trojans retreat into the city, Apollo reveals his
deception to Achilles, The death of Charles Nelson
Reilly, Fake out of Hector, The wickedness of Athena,
Worries about dogs, Hector bites the dust, Achilles'
bad behavior, Bad behavior of Greeks in general]**

While all this occurred on Troy's plain
The DeLorean took off in the rain.
Paris sighed
To Marty McFly
Said "I guess I'm back in the saddle again."

Said "I've read the Iliad you know,
And I guess were heading back through Time's flow
To save brother Hector."
McFly touched his pocket protector
Sighed, "The answer to that is a no."

Now Apollo reveals his deception.
And we really should make a correction.
If you look
It's in the previous book.
We lack all sense of direction.

But there is "No Direction Home-o"
As someone said. I think Perry Como
From now on we are linear
But always as tinny-eared
And we are nearing the end of out tome-o.

Achilles is caught up in the crud.
Garlic and sapphires there in the mud.
Apollo says "It's odd
You chasing a god."
Achilles says "If I could kill you, I would!"

Achilles ran like damned Smarty Jones
That day I watched at Malone's
Betting parlor.

You could hear me holler
Then despairingly run from the phones.

I took bets on that horse: Triple Crown
And watched as he lost. I was going down.
I said to the waiter.
"I hope I'll see you later."
Had a last drink and quickly skipped town.

Hector stood at the gate of the town.
Priam cries out then shouts down.
"Hector come home!
You're all alone!"
Hector don't make a sound.

Priam leans down and then calls
'Damn it dogs will be devouring my balls!"
It's there in the text
If you want to check.
And, man how that thought appalls.

Then, as old Homer attests
His mother wept and then bared her breasts.
"Come inside, son
Or we are undone.
This is a warning, this isn't a test."

Then Rod Serling had to make a decision.
Should he send in the Second Armored Division?
Which you could see
If you, like me.
Have "The Twilight Zone -- The Collector's Edition."

But Rod reluctantly has to say no.
Those tanks just had to go
To attack the Injun swarm
At the Little Big Horn
After all it's an American show.

Today when I got out of bed
I learned that Charles Nelson Reilly is dead.
But no time to grieve
I just gotta believe
"Drive" a certain poet once sd.

Oh the digressions are many
and most aren't worth half a penny.
Lets get back to the gates
where Hector awaits
some advice from his old pal, Jack Benny.

Jack said "Hector I might be wrong-a
But you shouldn't be here any longer
If you want to stay alive
Go down to track five.
The train's leaving for Anaheim, Azusa and Cucamonga.

But even though his poor parents begged
and pleaded, he wouldn't be plagued
with thoughts of his death.
No, he took a deep breath
and limbered his one creaky leg.

But, at last, he was truly undone
by the glint of A's bronze in the sun
as Achilles approached
he went white as a ghost
and took off on a dead run.

Oh then the horse race was on
with Achilles chasing Priam's scared son
'round the great walls of Troy
like a dog and a boy,
while the Gods just watched all the fun.

Zeus spoke first, saying, "Damn what a sight.
I thought Hector would put up a fight.
My heart fills with pity

when I think that his city
will be in big trouble tonight.

Then Zeus pulled out his damn scales,
and his ears heard the Trojan women's wails.
Hector's side was depressed,
and I'll bet you have guessed
that we're nearing the end of this tale.

And, please, we should never forget
The part that Athena played in it yet
It's so upsetting
That there's no regretting
Anything we have to regret.

Athena tricked the sad Trojan boy.
He looked to his left and ah, joy!
She pretended to be
His brother and he
Went down to the dark poor boy, poor boy.
Went down to the dark poor boy.

You see he thought his brother was there.
But it was just the queen of the air.
Achilles threw his spear
And though it went near
Hector danced from it like Fred Astaire.

Then Hector threw his own and it flew
To Achilles and almost went through
The god-given shield
But Achilles remained in the field
Saying "There's something you wish that you knew."

And he laughed as he brandished a spear
Said "Just to be perfectly clear.
This is the same one
And you thought I was undone
But Athena returned it, the dear!"

81

Then Hector turned to his brother
And asked him to give him another.
Then he realized
That he had idealized
The gods -- there wasn't a brother.

Hector said: "I am once more deceived
To think that I used to believe."
He took a breath
Said "Come ugly Death
Now there is no reprieve."

"The minstrel boy to the war has come-o"
He pulled his sword the scabbard from-o
Achilles thrust!
All mortals must
Pay the final sum-o

Poor Hector falls down to the dust.
Achilles boasts as you know he must.
Hector makes futile sounds
About not being fed to the hounds.
Achilles expresses his eternal disgust.

Achilles even says that he would
Eat him -- if he just only could.
He's a "man eater" quite
But no anthropophagite
But he doesn't want to be misunderstood.

So he alludes to the dogs and the birds
As Hector babbles forth words
Then twists the knife
And poor Hector's life
Utters the final absurds.

He tells Achilles he'll die at the gates.
Achilles replies that he scorns all the fates.

And with Hector's last breath
Achilles scorns death
And whatever whatsoever awaits.

And he said to all that would hear it,
"I did this for Patroclus' spirit."
Then he pierced Hector's heels,
hooked him up to his wheels
and dragged him around Troy's parapets.

Hecuba pulled out her hair.
Priam collapsed on the stair.
Andromache hears their wails,
she shakes, her skin pales.
Seeing Hector, her consciousness fails.

When she woke up she wept and decried
her son's fate, now father had died.
"Astyanax, my son
you'll soon be a bum,
when the Greeks and their horse get inside.

Book Twenty-Three
The Funeral Games for Patroclus

**[Tears Idle Tears, A visit from a spectre, A charming
request, Young men who remain in one immense
Body of Flame forming, for the moment, one of the
most brilliant spectacles ever witnessed!, The
impossibility of knowledge]**

The Greeks wanted to call the day quits
so they all went back to their ships.
But A and his Myrmidons
kept all their gear on
and rode up to Patroclus' kip.

And there they dismounted and wept
and Achilles touched Patroclus' breasts
saying, "Rest now in peace, friend
for Hector's met his end
and here he is, dog food at best."

Then the Greeks had a feast and a party
for Patroclus, that Achaean most arty.
There was blood, sweat and tears
they cooked pigs, sheeps and steers
and saw circus shows by Billy Barty.

As Achilles just moaned by the beach
the ghost of Patroclus came within reach
saying, "You must plant me soon,
Hades closes at noon."
Then something more strange as he beseeched:

"Achilles we've always been friends
and when, by the fates, your life ends,
mingle your ash and mine
in a jar amphorine
of the kind that your dear mother sends."

One last embrace Achilles sought
but reaching out, he found nought
but the cold midnight air
'neath the moon's vacant stare.
On they mourned the whole night, non-stop.

Then pink-fingered Dawn bumbled in
drinking a tonic and gin
saying "Whats all the fuss?
Get your butts on the bus!
Funeral games are about to begin!"

And Achilles slits the throats of of twelve teens
And then he insouciantly leans

While the Greeks play their game
Of immortal fame.
Nobody knows what it means.

Book Twenty-Four
A Sense of an Ending

**[Patroclus is dead and gone but Achilles keeps
hanging on, An aubade, A mother pleads to her son,
A father and a mule, Achilles and the many tricks to
evade the fulfillment of a common duty omitted, Chit
Chat, Eyebrows and Literature, Virtues of Hardin's
Domestic Medicine, Magnesia and an Eight O'Clock,
Hour Glasses and Pill Boxes, Egotism and Boiled
Eggs, The Funeral of Hector, Tamer of Horses
presented to the wonder and satisfaction of the
audience, Positively the Last Night!!!!!!!!!!!!!!]**

Though Patroclus is dead and gone
Achilles just hangs on and on.
He can't let him go
so he weeps, full of woe
from sunset till golden robed Dawn.

His treatment of Hector is vile
and it bugs the gods after a while.
A's mother, Thetis
tells him, "Don't be defeatest
there isn't much time on the dial."

So he agrees to give Hector back
to anyone who comes with a pack
of jewels, gold or wine
any one will be fine
as long as they bring a big stack.

Hector's dad says, "Dammit I'll go.
For his death has been quite a blow.
Go get me a basket
And a mule for his casket
Hurry up now, I'm late for the show."

Hermes guides Priam on down.
Achilles says "You do get around.
You can have your son
But you still better run."
Priam takes the body to town.

The Trojans go out and get wood
because Achilles said they could.
Then Hector was roasted
as to the gods they all toasted
then buried his ashes for good.

And everyone a grand sentiment endorses.
And the stars proceed in their courses
As per usual
Such is the funeral
Of Hector, Tamer of Horses

Book Twenty-Five
From There to Eternity

The DeLorean came down to the plain
And Paris stepped out in the rain.
Then no rain. No Troy city.
No town without pity.
And nothing beside remains.

"Did I kill Achilles or what?"
Marty says "Don't know I guess I forgot.
But look up! Two moons!"
And out of the ruins

Stepped the cast of Camelot.

And Paris saw Helen there!
Smiling and touching her hair.
Said Marty McFly
"If you want to know why..."
The lovers touched. "I guess I don't care."

Paris asked "Was it all a dream?"
And they all disappeared in a beam
Of violet starlight
They disappeared into the night.
A Love Supreme! A Love Supreme!

Only Marty was standing there
Then Doc Brown appeared from no where.
Doc: "We gotta go!"
Marty: "Yeah, Doc, I know
Into the DeLorean back into Time's Flow."

Straight to the heart of Lyra.

So that:

Epilogue

This is the end of the Limerick Iliad
Which flowed like the Balm of Gilead
If your vision's dim
Blame Joe or Tim
Who are just two guys -- not a myriad.

The Limerick Odyssey

Book One

Telemachus

[Loomings, When Homer Smote His Bloomin' Lyre, Odysseus -- His questionable character, Following Homer much is revealed anent the Oxen of the Sun allowing us to skip this later, Athena to Telemachus, Who's Your Daddy?, Gallants doomed, A Son Upbraids His Mother]

It all begins with Calypso
Who is bit of a witch so
Odysseus stays
In Media Res
Hence it follows facto ipso

That there's no invoking the Muse,
a treatment to which she's not used.
But Homer scoffs
And laughs it off
Which makes many very confused.

Now one of us is a bit of a souse
And the other a bit of a louse
But it's been decided
And we're quite excited
We will use the translation of W.H.D. Rouse.

A fellow who was verrrry British
Though his translation is merely middish
He pursued "strange love"
Which was clearly enough
To make parsons and dons very skittish.

And he seemed to be on a mission
And he had made a strange decision
The servants all talk
Like poor, Irish sots
And the gods like British patricians.

And though it seems wrong and ridiculous
To claim that Odysseus was somewhat TravisBickleous
We're making that claim
In the Muse's name
Who knows everything is quite fickleous.

The Iliad Odysseus is a bore
This has been suggested before
A bit of a lout
And an evil scout
Back in the Trojan war.

Take a look at the after action report,
If presented at the Nuremberg court.
It would most surely follow
That the blade or the gallows
Would be O's final reward.

But he lies in the arms of Calypso
Who is a nympho and dipso
A most ample goddess
Who fills out her bodice
And wears her hair in a most cunning flip-o.

Ah, but you can see what the diff is:
He's not the same Odysseus:
In the Iliad -- a piss ant

In the Odysssey a soi-disant
Hero who misses his missus.

And her name isn't Calypso
Who doesn't seem to give a rip-o.
About the wife over the sea
Patient Penelope:
"Brave Odysseus just have another sip-o!

For why go down to your ship?
Come dear, let me taste of your lips."
And who really knows
Just how it goes?
I heard a rumor of leather and whips.

Odysseus -- lost all companions
Underneath the magnolias and banyans
Of the Isle of the Sun
What had they done?
Their shades cry out from the canyons

Of Hades and the constant topic
Of the gods who are quite heliotropic
Is "Poor brave Odysseus
What a pity this is
That Poseidon can't be more philanthropic."

After all he said "This won't do.
The oxen of the sun ain't for you."
But they were starving
And acted like Lee Marvin
Would have done in the flick "Cat Ballou."

They roasted those big boys on a spit
And naturally those cowpokes got hit.
They were dry-gulched:
How will not be divulged
Until later -- when we'll get to it.

Now Poseidon was among the Ethiopians
Who loved him and were helitropian.
He ate bulls and rams
Country sausages and hams
In that land across the sea Fallopian.

You must remember Agamemnon
Remembered by many penmen:
He was murdered most foully
By a vile Svengali
Who up and stole Agamemnon's woman.

Zeus spake and said "Little gods, oh, please.
We told Aegisthus he would be killed by Orestes
But the fellow went his way
As if we had no say
Though the messages was delivered by dear Hermes."

But Athena interrupted Father Zeus:
Said "Sometimes I think it is no use.
But what about Odysseus
Faithful and fastidious
Can't we help him and declare a truce?"

Zeus sighed, "How the times do beteem us
But, as gods, I think t'would beseem us
To forget and forgive
And let Odysseus live
Despite what he did to Polyphemus.

Besides, that fellow's quite horrid
One's sensibilities often feel jarred
He lives in a cave
And is an ill-mannered knave
And has one eye in the middle of his forehead.

And now that one eye is blind.
True, Odysseus was quite unkind
Since after he blinded him

He then reminded him
That he had the superior mind

But the gods always like a fine jest-o
And Odysseus should be forgiven all lest-o
We want the rumor
That we have no sense of humor
To spread. I think that is best-o.

And, frankly to Hell with my brother.
Ganymede! I'll have another!
Yes, the Cyclop's the son
Of poor Poseidon
But if we can't take a joke, then why bother?"

Athena said "Send Hermes Argeiphontes
With some Special Forces and Mounties
To Tell Calypso
To let Odysseus go
He's not just one of her dandies!

And since we don't want the mortals to mock us
Let me go down to see Telemachus!"
Zeus nodded consent
And Athena went.
Zeus looked around and hollered for Bacchus.

Then clapped his hands and all became smoke
And he was in Tokyo and had a few tokes.
He loved karaoke
And though he sang off key
Sang an ironic version of "I Started a Joke."

Athena put on her ruby red slippers
Then flew down past both of the Dippers.
A goddess, she went as
And old fellow named Mentes
Who had just arrived on a fine Yankee clipper.

The goddess stood at the gate
And, impertinently was made to wait
By those balloxing boozers
Penelope's suitors
Who roared out foul limericks as they ate

Barrels of eels from the larder
Fine buffalo steaks tartare
And when they did dine
They had six hundred flagons of wine.
And would not behave as they oughta.

And there was Odysseus's son
Who hated them everyone
Who greeted him as politely
As Holly Golightly
But wasn't having any fun.

He told Mentes the suitors were phonies
As they dined on fresh abalones.
Asked "Say, do you know
Just where the ducks go?"
In a rather listless monotoni.

"I see you're sensitive kid.
And you keep your true feelings well hid.
What would you say
If I told you one day
You're Dad's gonna squash them like squids?"

At this Telemachus was more cheerful
And Mentes gave him and earful
Said, "Your Dad is detained
And has likely remained
Thinking of you and most tearful.

He has recently descended to Hades
On behalf of all gallants and ladies
And he'll be right home

He has freed Persephone
And is somewhere in the Southern Cyclades!"

Then up jumped Telemachus with glee
Said "Now I am going to sea!"
And ran up the stairs
A man of affairs
Scorning the petite bourgeoisie.

Then the night began to lower:
The time known as "The Children's Hour"
Between dark and daylight
Athena took flight
And flew to the Martello Tower.

She stopped to try to cheer up Rilke
Then got some clothes from the Fiddler of Dee
While Dedalus waited
And micturated
Into the snot-green sea.

At the last I think the scene is
T's mom and the singer Phemius.
He is singing the blues
Or am I confused?
What I seem to want to mean is

He's singing many sad verses
About husbands gone way in black hearses
And sailors that drown
The whole world around
And die spewing many vile curses.

And Penelope says "Oh desist!
And Telemachus seizes her wrist
And cries out "Play On!"
And quotes Francois Villion
Then takes the lyre and plays some Franz Liszt.

He plays the Mazurka brillante.
Then plays it again andante.
Sends his Mom to her room.
Then we may assume
Breaks into an obscene Greek cante.

Book Two
Telemachus Prepares for His Voyage

**[Telemachus summons all the Achaeans to an
assembly, Homer's Obsessions, Joyce even stranger,
The thonging and bonging of a likely lad, The suitors
mock Telemachus, The Queen of the Fairies tells
Telemachus to find the ONE RING]**

Dawn came with "fingers of rose."
That's a mistake I suppose.
But Homer is dead
And like James Joyce said
About "The Dead" -- well, nobody knows.

Telemachus get ups and dresses.
What did he wear? Homer's best guesses
Are a Harry Potter tee shirt
And a sharp sword that he girt
O'er his shoulders, then Homer obsesses

Over the appearance of the young fellow's feet
Which he describes as "shining." You'll meet
By my guesses
No greater foot fetishist
In literature. Homer's damn hard to beat.

But James Joyce had a fetish more rare:
He would take his wife Nora's underwear
And in a Parisian cafe

With them would dally and play.
It was shocking but he just didn't care.

For as he played he looked through Time's portal
And what he saw would cause him to chortle
"I see I surpass
Poor Homer, alas,
Back asswards insures I'm immortal."

There are problems in poor Homer's text
For Homer goes on to what's next
And we must assume
That the young man left his room
With no pants -- and remain somewhat vexed.

And this is undoubtedly wrong.
Let's assume he is wearing a thong
To prevent his young testicles
From becoming a spectacle,
And over all he casts a sarong.

And then he puts on his glasses.
Don't give me your historical whereases
For I find
That he was nearly blind
And, damn it, he needed those glasses.

Then he took a last look at his room.
This Homer neglects but I assume
Since he will be a Man
We may understand
The poor old toys he has left behind loom.

He rushes out but I think he would care
If he knew that his old Teddy Bear
With the one glass eye
Sobbed and asked why
Telemachus was leaving him there.

And goodbye pornographic papyruses
And the hot priestesses he used to admire. It is
A fact
That Balling the Jack
All alone is a teenage requireusus.

One thing he was determined to bring:
His Little Orphan Annie Decoder ring!
Who know what Fate bodes
And what sorts of strange codes
He would need to decipher? "Ping! Ping!"

It was R2D2 and old C3PO!
Indicating that they'd like to go.
But he left them behind.
I think he will find
That there will be a time he will need them you know!

Into a sea bag he thrust Daddy's old photo
And left his mother a note on his desk. Oh,
Will he be unkind
And leave his best friend behind?
No! Into the bag jumped dear Toto!

Telemachus said "Don't make a sound."
Picked up the bag and then looked around
For a few books to take
To keep him awake
When he was Cyclades bound.

"I think I'll take Harry Potter
To read while crossing the water."
The other books he brings
Are "The Lord of the Rings"
And "The Young Gentleman's Guide to Slaughter."

He left behind his record collection
Which was quite good -- there was a whole section
Devoted to Emo

But now he was Primo
And was heading in a different direction.

Then he went to a secret drawer
And pulled out a Colt .44.
It was anachronistic
But he was realistic
Why else was he his father's son for?

He put the gun and ammo 'neath his sarong
And fastened them to him with a strong thong.
Then left his boyhood behind
His father to find
And he hummed an old nautical bong song.

He stepped into the hall with great pep.
He looked just like a young Johnny Depp
And he busted out singing
Because he was beginning
At last to establish his rep.

He called airily to some damn old servant
Said "Listen now at your master's urging.
Call all the long-haired Achaeans
And the short-haired Fakeyones
To assemble at once. Yes, it's urgent!"

This is Homer and so you know soon
We're gonna meet some slippered pantaloon.
Homer won't gyp us.
His name is Aegyptius
He comes in humming a familiar tune.

His son had been eaten by the Cyclops
And he had been a member of "The Four Tops"
And his Daddy was down
With the best of Motown
And sang "Sugar Pie, Honey Bunch" with re-bops.

So they all patiently waited.
They all understood it was fated.
He sang "Are You Man Enough?
Calling his bluff.
A tune the boy always hated.

Then Telemachus sang of his Papa
First Country then Soft Rock then Rappa
And everyone sighed
"Oh, my Daddy died
And my Mom's suitors are eating my supper."

Then Telemachus was given the sceptre
All of a sudden it was as if the spectre
Of his Pater Familias
Pissed off and bilious
Was back in the Ithaca sector.

He denounces all the suitors as parasites
Vile usurpers who have taken his rights
And he promises soon
Neath the bad rising moon
They will have some terrible nights.

And most of those bastards were cowed
Only Antinous spoke up from the crowd
Said "Telemachus you boaster
I see your face on a poster
Of sons who are weakly endowed.

Do you think you, little fellow, can scare us?
Your father would be quite embarrassed.
And you know your Mom
Has been putting us on.
So why do you strut and dare us?

She responds to our billet doux:
"Dear young man, I am thinking of you!
But now you must wait

Hang about at the gate
For I have something to do!"

And then she goes up to her room
And works for a bit on her loom
Making a shroud
And singing out loud
Of Laertes and his doom.

She said to each one of us, "Please
I must weave a shroud for Laertes!
And when we are done
We will have such fun!"
She's acting like a bitch and a tease!

For every damn night we are told
She betrays the promise she sold
She unravels the thread
And then goes to bed
Betraying we suitors so bold!

There's only one thing that you now can do
And you're lucky that I'm telling you
Send you Mom to her father
Who will tell he she oughta
Do what he tells her to do.

And marry one of us and tout de suite
That we may caress her fair feet
And fondle her delicates footsies
And all her tootsies.
Tell her to stop this deceit!"

Homer may need some sexual healing.
Am I alone in that feeling?
This obsession with feet
I have to repeat
Is not so very appealing.

"I'm a man so, of course, I'm her boss
But do you think for a minute I'd toss
Out my dear mater?
To marry one of you later?"
Telemachus replied giving his head a toss.

And then -- nobody knows why
Two great eagles appeared in the sky.
They dive bombed the crowd
And squawked really loud
Then disappeared in the sweet bye and bye.

And how the crowd was impressed
And augur stood up. Said he guessed
First there would be an eclipse
Then an apocalypse
Then a flood and they all would regret

All of the names that they called him
And all of the times that they stalled him
When he asked for a dime
To buy Thunderbird wine
Then the crowd grew impatient and mauled him.

Then Zeus sent a California condor
On its back was a Princess of Gondor
And she was totally nude
Imbued with intense pulchritude
Although her hair might have been a tad blonder.

A great silence came over the swarm
And they began to feel uncomfortably warm
And they ran to the sea
And behaved exceedingly free
But the suitors slunk back to the dorm.

For the poor fellows had been made to swear
To Aphrodite and how they regretted it there
To abstain from all lust

Until one of them must
Win sweet Penelope the Fair.

And, of course, this explains their frustration
And the poor fellows' incessant masturbation
It was an odd oath
And, by my troth,
A disgrace to the whole Grecian nation.

Aphrodite herself was a maniac
And, of course, didn't need an aphrodisiac
But she thought it exciting
To keep on inciting
These fellows to increasingly zany acts.

Then suddenly the day went all darkling
And poor little Toto was barkling.
T. went down to the sea
To ponder and pee
When he saw an auspicious sparkling.

It was enough to unman ya.
"Hello, my name's Titania
And the main thing
Is...you have the One Ring!"
T. said, "I don't quite understand ya.

The One Ring should make me invisible!"
Titania replied "That is quite risible
And is simply a sign
You have read too much Tolkien.
The One Ring makes you feel miserable."

T. said "Then I guess you are right.
But I can't get it off. It's too goddman tight."
"This isn't a test
You must go on a quest,"
Said the fairy. And she was quite forthright.

T. almost broke down right there.
Said "Goddammit I guess you're aware..."
But she had a system
And bent down and kissed him
Then murmured and stroked his dark hair.

Then suddenly he was so far!
He gave a shout! He was crossing the bar
In a brave brigadoon
Beneath the mysterious moon
And following a westering star.

Book Three
Telemachus Visits Nestor in Pylos

**[Into the mysterious Omphalus, Telemachus,
depressed, dreams, Muscle Beach, An episode Homer
neglects to mention, George Burns seeking Gracie
Allen]**

"Ho!" he cried. "Westward to Pylos.
Into the mysterious Omphalus"
He was ahead of himself: he
Knew the Omphalus is at Delphi.
He was only heading to old Nestor's palace.

But he felt he was in great danger
And surrounded by mysterious strangers
An elven crew
What would he do
If out from the hold strode the Ranger?

Yes, Aragorn -- known to many as Strider
He also felt pursued by a mysterious rider.

But this is the Odyssey:
Cyclops and wine-dark sea
It's not the book of a paperback writer.

Besides, the poor fellow had little choice.
Homer based everything on James Joyce.
And something faded away
At the dawn of the day
When he heard a familiar voice.

On the deck...why it was just Mentor
And he stood on the deck in the center
Surrounded by Greeks,
No elvish freaks.
"There isn't even a centaur."

And Telemachus was, at once, depressed
Went down to the cabin, undressed
Put away his things
Started reading "Lord of the Rings"
As the brigantine kept heading west.

And he dreamt of another career
In the sorta Middle-Earth sphere
He thought "After all
Our gods are so dull."
He felt he might not persevere.

And Athena was proving this true.
After all what did that goddess do?
She was disguised as Mentor
She was of that bent, her
Jejune notions never under review.

I wonder if there was a time when
Someone said to Homer "Again?"
And walked out of the room
And dreamt of Barsoom
But to get back to out story, then

The ship arrived and there on the sand
Was Nestor with a samba band
And the usual crew
To do what they do:
Killing bulls for Poseidon the Grand.

Telemachus was snoozing with Toto
When Mentor suggested he go to
The deck.
T. said "What the heck"
And tried to recover his mojo.

There were 900 times 5 on the beach
And all calling each to each
And dining on tripe
And bullocks and snipe
But no one was eating a peach.

Yes, there were nine groups of 500 on the beach
And everyone calling each to each
They were devouring entrails
And guzzling wine served in pails
Conveniently placed within reach.

There was a chapel to scrapple
And there the Pylosites would dapple
Their lips with the entrails
Of bullocks and whales
And with huge thigh bones would grapple.

The young man's heart was a-rending
Because at this time he was tending
To be a contrarian
And a strict vegetarian
And, besides, he was bullockbefriending.

But Mentor just shouted "Let's go!
This is the kingdom of Nestor you know

And he will be glad
Because he liked your Dad."
But Telemachus closed his eyes and said "No."

Then tried to think of excuses.
And said to Mentor "The truth is
I'm shy
And Nestor's such a tough guy
I don't really know what the use is."

For he had spied the King on the sand
And he was doing pushups -- with only one hand
Up and down went his weenie
Poking from his bikini
Which couldn't contain his huge kingly gland.

For deep within old Nestor's palace
Was the most potent sort of Cialis
Given to Nestor
By a satyr named Lester
In a topless bar down in West Dallas.

"Ah, Mentor tell me...my guess is
Those nude fellows doing bench presses
In a sort of a ring
Almost surrounding the King
Are the princes (a thought which depresses)."

And Mentor said "You're damn right-o!
Look at their pecs -- and they can fight-o!
But Telemachus sighed
And he almost cried.
Damn it -- something just wasn't right-o.

Was he really the son of Odysseus?
His build was closer to the Genus Sissyus.
He thought himself "imperially slim"
But the joke was on him.
This engendered an adolescent crisius.

He shivered there in the sea breeze.
Athena could sense his unease.
But he grew bolder
When she touched his shoulder.
He appeared like a young Hercules!

And, of course she thought it'd be way cool
Though some might think it quite cruel:
She transformed Toto
Into a proto
Two headed six-balled Pit Bull.

"My name is Rambo Telemachuspous
And I have strength of a Cantabrigian catapultapous
I roam strange lands
And I've come to these sands
Sent by the Sanctimonious Octopus.

My hound's name is Chrysanthropus Chrysalis.
We come bearing the sign of the phallus.
Greetings great King.
Of thee we sing
In the suburbs of Far Western Dallas."

The speech seems a tad bit inflated
But Athena patiently waited.
There was a pause.
Then several rounds of applause.
T's rhetoric seemed highly rated.

"I come to you seeking my Papa
And, so sorry, this is just a brief stop
A word of Odysseus
(This bull's thigh's delicious)
And I'm off to seek my dear Papa."

King Priam bounded over the sand
And took Telemachus by the hand.

"You? You're the one?
You're that dear man's son?
Come here sweet boy! This is grand."

Priam's face was bewrinkled. His hair grizzled.
But the rest of him was perfectly chiseled.
And all those Cilaises
Had given him four pectoralisis
And what looked like a giant bull's pizzle.

And he called out to his lieges and vassals
To drink up and cry out many wassails
There was a great vox humana
As they went to the cabana
He explained it was his summer castle.

He lounged there on a fine throne
Looking quite like Sylvester Stallone
And said "Oh, my boy.
I will tell you of Troy."
Then he wept and gave a low moan.

"Your Daddy has been in my prayers
Last time I saw him he was bare assed
He had a dose
From the Priestess of Kos
Ah, we were a fine bunch of slayers.

Did you know that after old Troy was sacked-o
Your daddy said he'd turn back-o
We were already at sea
Some of the guys and me
Oh, so many got whacked-o.

You Dad said he'd rejoin the King
Which was, I'm afraid, the wrong thing
For the King was at Troy
And that seemed to annoy
Poseidon who promised he'd bring

All sorts of troubles and woes
You Dad said "Well that's the way that it goes."
And he turned back
With a complete lack of tact
With a boatful of varlets and ho's.

Your father seemed -- can I say-- strangely changed
And more than a little deranged
And a strange entertainment
Showed his derangement
At nights on the boat he arranged

Something he called "Vaudeville."
I don't understand it and I never will
He stood on the stage
A man of his age…
With a Phrygian trollop named Lil.

He wore a strange hat. Had a cane.
And what he did next seemed insane
He danced and he burbled
About a lost love named "Myrtle"
While the trollop was shakin' her thang.

He stopped and told terrible jokes
Referred to his warriors as "mokes"
Then did a lewd dance
While that trollop did prance
Until and enchanted pig said "That's all folks!"

Then the heaven's began to thunder
And the pig admitted his blunder
And Odysseus came back
With another strange act:
Baby Alice the Midget Wonder!

This went on for nine nights
And during each night there appeared a strange light

A ray from star
That moved here and thar
As they danced and sang in delight.

On the ninth night we were sipping sauternes--
On the deck. I expressed my concerns
Then down from a star
Came a strange god with a cigar.
Odysseus said. "By the gods--that's George Burns!"

Who said "You think I'm God -- prima facie
But I think God is Count Basie.
Here have a cigar.
I got to get back to that star.
I'm still looking for Gracie."

Then your father --if you'd seen his face--
Said "That's it I must go find Grace!"
The jumped over the bow
And climbed up the prow
Of his ship -- and left with no a trace.

My guess is that your Dad is at sea
Suffering from PTSD.
Perhaps there's more to find out.
Go ask Menelaus.
And now let's talk about me!"

Which he did until Dawn's rosy fingers
Suggested that they should not linger.
Then they hopped on a freight
That stopped at Track 8
To pick up some Singapore slingers.

Book Four
Telemachus Visits Menelaus in Sparta

**[The giraffe offered as a token of what is to come,
"A" Train to Sparta, Helen in the Twilight Zone,
How Troy Fell,]**

They arrived at the House of Menelaus-o.
And I remember Picasso
Said with a laugh
That besides the giraffe
God seriously fucked up so.

But this is back when the old world was young:
Back before even Homer had sung:
There was an innocent glisteria
On the lilacs and wisteria
And gods walked mortals among.

And one could get away with that sentence
And really feel no repentance.
But poetic style
Decayed all the while
Poets lost their compos mentis.

And now it's devolved to the blog
And the croakings of floggers and flogged
Be still my heart.
We need to make a new start:
Where the Southern crosses the Yellow Dog.

They jumped off the train at Sparta
I really feel that I lack the art-a
To be very specific
That would be terrific
But I find I do not give a fart-a.

For instance I lack the divine afflatus
To mention Priam's son Peisistratus
He hung with with T.
And he went with he

To the palace wherever that is.

They were having a wedding feast.
Menelaus's brother was already deceased
Helen was back
In Menelaus's rack
Since the Trojan war had ceased.

She said the whole time she was sad
And drugged and possibly mad
And had only one love
And was thoroughly sick of
The rumors that alleged she was bad.

Of course, she ain't the real Helen
Although she had magnificent melons.
She came from Macys, New York
Was designed by a fellow named Bjork
And her real name was Ellen.

I suppose you want to know more.
It begins on Macy's ninth floor
To buy a gold thimble
She had gone to Gimbels
But they didn't have any no more.

Ah, it is such a strange interlude:
The saleslady is rather rude
She complains of all this,
(how she does moan and piss)
and thus she is forced to conclude

That she is in the Twilight Zone
And she feels so terribly alone
And can't keep her panic in!
She finds out she's a mannequin
And that her cover is blown.

And, of course, the episode ends

And Rod Serling says "Goodnight friends"
And I went to bed
A ten year old sleepy head
Not guessing what it all portends.

Because at that moment and out of the sky
Came Paris and Marty McFly.
She felt euphorian
In the back of the DeLorean
As they told her the what where and why.

They dropped her off as Troy was falling
And Menelaus was desperately calling
For his dear Helen
And her magnificent melons
And she rushed to his arms and began bawling.

And she seemed so loving and possessive
Though sometimes she seemed quite obsessive
A demanding neurotic
But strangely erotic
And often mannequin depressive.

Now, just as the confab was starting,
(This is an epic and you might find this disheartening)
Because of the meat
He had been forced to eat
Telemachus couldn't stop farting.

Menelaus said "I have just one suggestion."
T. moaned "Sorry, I have indigestion."
But Menelaus faced him
And then he embraced him.
"You are Odysseus's son without any question!

"I suggest that we walk in the park."
And they did and talked until dark.
And T remained gaseous
And alas and alack he is

The death of many a linnet and lark.

But Menelaus was nothing but kind.
Said, "You see, I don't really mind.
Your ghastly gaseousness
Is noble not crasseous
I love your Pappa's behind!

You've heard of the famed Trojan Horse?"
T. replied "My man, but of course!
My father and others
Oh that bold band of brothers
Hid inside then with o'er whelming force..."

Menelaus said, "There were no others inside
Only your father inside did slide
And there passing gas
From his noble ass
Did he for nine days abide!

The Trojans took the horse in the city
And he keep on farting with no pity
Then on the tenth day
During Priam's soiree
The trapdoor was found by a Trojan committee.

And that unleased a deadly miasma
That turned many Trojans to plasma.
And all that were left
Were a few Trojans bereft
And suffering from severe cases of asthma.

But my dear Helen seemed immune
And we embraced beneath a glowing Spring moon
We were inured to the scent
Because of our noble descent
But my sweet breath caused her to swoon.

She strangely seemed somewhat rigid

But she explained she was frigid
As a clever ruse
That she did use
To keep Paris away from her widget."

I think it would be quite odious
To describe Menelaus's fight with Proteus
As Homer does
Simply because
He wishes to be quite commodious.

So this is the end of Book Four
Which seems like an awful damn bore:
Mostly prolusion
And very confusin'
As I've mentioned before.

Book Five
Odysseus Leaves Calypso's Island and Reaches
Phaeacia

[Go tell it on the mountain "Let my Odysseus go!"
Calypso frees her man, The First Internal
Combustion Engine, Reaches Phaeacia]

Go tell it on the mountain, over the hill and
everywhere.
Go tell it on the mountain, to let Odysseus go.

Who's that yonder dressed in red? Let my Odysseus
go.
Must be Calypso like I already said.
Let my Odysseus go!

Go tell it on Olympus

Here there and everywhere.
Tell them that the gods do pimp us.
Unless they let my Odysseus go!

On Olympus they had a Gospel Choir
And they sang as the banged on their lyres
As they sang they grooved
Sang "We will not be moved!"
Like Abyssinian Baptists from Cairo.

Zeus just sneered. Said, "Maybe later."
Even when they sang about John the Revelator
But he began to get down
When out came James Brown.
"Who's that magnificent satyr?"

And that's how it all got done:
Cause of Soul Brother Number One
Zeus stopped being a drag.
Poppa's got a brand new bag
And he said to Hermes "Go, run!"

Zeus steps down from his Tower of Power
And does the Funky Chicken for an hour
Shouts out for Jolene
Sings "I'm a Sex Machine!"
As the goddesses cower in their bower.

Calypso has no choice but to obey
Though she calls Zeus one messed up ofay.
She tells Odysseus fast
Go build a raft
And clear out by the end of the day.

Odysseus bangs his raft together
While humming, I think, "Stormy Weather."
Calypso just turns
And ask him when he returns
To being her Spanish boots of Spanish Leather.

Odysseus treats her quite nice
Then stokes up on red beans and rice
Says "I gave you my heart
But you wanted my soul
But don't think twice, it's all right."

Then he drags the raft the ocean.
Then begins to put it in motion.
With one's ass in the water
An accomplished farter
Can generate smooth locomotion.

He passes gas faster and faster.
He is an accomplished master.
Red beans and rice
Will always suffice
To avoid a nautical disaster!

Athena looks down and says "Boss,
He's a real man -- never at a loss."
But Zeus didn't care
Because he wasn't there
He was a concubinin' with the Priestess of Kos.

But, of course, Poseidon tries to drown him
His favorite hobby is to hound him
But Odysseus is saved
And on a quite splendid wave:
Washes up just where Nausicaa found him.

And it's important to note he is nude
And, apparently completely screwed
In a strange land
Under the command
Of a King who might be quite rude.

Book Six
Odysseus and Nausicaa

[What happened to Nausicaa]

Nausicaa was the daughter of Alcinous
Who was the King so that makes her a princess
She was sweet and demure
But that was before
She dabbled with herbal hair rinses.

She had hair like the black Kalamata
And she had been a sweet little daughter
But one day she reached
For a rinse and got bleach
And it wouldn't come out in the water.

Suddenly she was a bleached blonde
And seemed transformed as if with a wand
Instead of a sweet little la la
She became something like Zsa Zsa
And longed to join the Beau Monde.

But she was stuck in the Kingdom of Scheria,
Mostly prairie and definitely nary a
High end boutique
Or Valentino like sheik
bent on breaking the laws of Sharia.

All of the Scheria bon ton
Consisted of her family and a certain swan
Whose, rumor had it,
Patootie had been patted
By Zeus in days far long gone.

So, she lay reading Teen Glamour
And dreaming of a high society amour

And thought it was right
When she heard that night
That Paris Hilton was getting out of the slammer.

And here Homer simply repeats
That she went to the river to wash sheets
Led by a dream-a
Sent by Athena
A rumor repeated by Keats.

And there she met the big guy
Naked. And she seemed so shy
And sweetly did blush
As he came out of the bush
And quite innocently did sigh.

But that's not the way it went down.
She was thinking I gotta get out of this town
When Athena suggested
When she felt quite rested
She put on her best Gucci gown.

"For near the beach and nude you will see
The flower of the aristocracy
Brave Odysseus
Whose both Damon and Pythias
The height of all myth he is
Just in from the isle of Capri!"

So she runs as fast as she can
Expecting a dashing fellow out of Rodin
When he comes out of the bush
She doesn't blush
But cries "Oh, who is this farting old man???"

And Nausicaa is so damn shocked
That significant passions are unlocked
She ends up with Sappho
Sharing a laugh-oh!

As the strange ways of men are mocked.

She sends her servant for a mule.
"Go ahead, take that old fool
Away to the palace
I'm off to see Alice
Toklas. I think she is cool."

Book Seven
Odysseus at the Court of Alcinous in Phaeacia

**[Odysseus invents the Banjo, Attacked by the Klan,
His ass saved by the International Brotherhood of
Railway Porters, to the Spouter Inn, Ahab not an
Arab]**

But Odysseus maintains savoir-faire
Everything solid melts in the air.
But he ain't feeling too well
So he takes two Di-Gel
Says "Go ahead I'll follow you there."

Thinks "Passing gas at will is a plus
(That's how Vaudeville came down to us.)
But I need something new."
So what did he do?
(Three paragraphs at least. Discuss).

Well, back in the bush he did go.
A dead cat was there don't you know.
And he took out his sword
And hollowed out a gourd
And invented the five string banjo.

The strings were made of catgut
And he stretched them till they did abut

One end of a board
Fastened to the hollowed out gourd
And they were attached by cut monkey nuts.

Things soon all fell into place.
Then he bent down with no little grace,
Rubbed his face in the mud
Like a Tennessee stud
And walked down the road in blackface.

He began to play Cotton-Eyed Joe
And then another melody we know
And he heard an echo
And turned his neck-o
Somebody else was playing "Dueling Banjos."

There on the Chattahoocieapolis Bridge it
Looked like a malevolent midget.
As Odysseus played
He felt made in the shade
He could play like an Appalacianoupolis idjit!

But was it all a plot to distract him?
He was feeling so fine when they attacked him.
He wasn't the first blackface man
To be attacked by the Klan
And the yellow dogs of both parties backed them!

He turns and cries out to the gods
Buy what happened next may seem odd:
The Black Abyssinian Church
Made from Olympus a lurch
And laid those bastards under the sod.

Ant least a hundred went down
Under the diamond head cane of James Brown
And at least a quarter
Were done in by railroad porters
With whatever was laying around.

And there was a legion of gay Unitarians
Led by a transsexual Rasatfarian
They laid them all low
Then said they had to go
To a performance of "Rent" up in Darien.

And they meant Darien, Connecticut
For they insisted on a certain etiquette
They would all take their places
With clean clothes and bright faces
Just as in "Socrates is a man" "is a man" is the predicate.

So they missed the soft shoe by Bojangles
And how Odysseus was shown all the angles
Of fair minstrelsy
Near the Aegean sea
As the bridge at midnight dangles.

So he arrives at the palace's gate
In the know but really quite late.
But he had the nerve
And thought "They also serve
Who have a banjo and stand and wait."

So he stood outside played "Natchez Under the Hill"
Then "Pretty Little Miss Jump in the Well"
Then he went back
In a claw hammer attack
Played "I Had an Old Dog Named Bill."

Then he moved down to in front of the Marriot
But only the guy parking the chariots
Gave him a drachma
Following the dogma
That only the proletariat helps the proletariat.

Homer says Odysseus sees the King.
But he didn't: he didn't have any bling

And a man in blackface
Don't get to that place
No matter how cool he's shakin' his thing.

So he went down to the Spouter Inn
And a sailor bought him a gin
Said "My name is Queequeg
You look like you need a new gig.
What was your name again?"

Odysseus looked at him said "Hell,
You can go ahead and call me Ishmael
I'm a stranger here
And I fear
I ain't doing too well."

Book Eight
Odysseus is Entertained in Phaeacia

[Book Eight by Homer is a lie]

Book Eight by Homer is a lie.
Obviously you now know why.
Odysseus never talked to the King
He did no such thing.
It was at the Spouter Inn he did sigh

Getting drunk with a headhunting sailor
Who was getting ready to get aboard a whaler.
Yes, the Pequod.
Which seems quite odd
And like something from Norman Mailer.

So just go on and read the next book
Please appreciate the trouble we took
To bring you at last

To all the adventures that passed
Independent of the usual gobbledygook.

Book Nine
Ismarus, the Lotus Eaters, and the Cyclops

[The Cicones, Seaman Schliemann , The Cyclops.]

And just as he was about to begin
A man named Ahab came in.
Yes, he was Ahab
But not Ahab the Arab
Cause he ordered twelve rounds of gin.

"Tomorrow," he cried, "We set sail
To find Moby Dick the white whale
So, let's all have some drinks
Before we go after the Sphinx
And listen to the tale of this man Ishmael!"

Then the crew sauntered into the bar
If you're a reader, you know who they are
There was Billy Budd
And old Captain Blood
And some ghosts from the Second World War.

Odysseus took a great slug of gin
Said, "Gentlemen, I'm about to begin
But let's first have a song
So we don't go wrong."
And they all sang "The Mighty Quinn."

Then the door flew open! What rough beast!
They sensed the supernatural at the least.
But it was the final three
Of the Beau Jeste's company:

A minister, a rabbi and a priest.

"There once was a wench from Connecticut
Who had Old Glory under her petticut
When she was asked why
She said I don't know but I
Believe in following Connecticut etiquette."

If Odysseus expected a laugh,
He had committed a gaffe.
These fellows looked intensely
Like they cared immensely
For the Tale Proper and to hell with the chaff!

So he began. And for what it's worth
He began absent all mirth
And started out quite basso
"This," he said "also
Has been one of the dark places of the earth.

My name is Odysseus Laertiades
I've been all around even to Hades
Been to Hell and Back
That's simply a fact.
But that don't help me with the ladies.

I fought in the old Trojan war
Heaps of nothing, heaps of gore.
When I left
I felt quite bereft.
I wondered "Why" and What For"

I thought "Man, there's got to be something more."
I been down to the killing floor.
I felt bad till
I invented "Vaudeville."
No, it weren't invented by Al Gore.

But I'm gonna tell the tale straight.

Why me? Why was this my Fate?
It's a tale of wonders
And many blunders
And it begins at Troy Gate.

Troy destroyed. I just wanted to head home.
I felt like the hero of some epic poem:
Doomed to wander
Because of an unspecified blunder,
Doomed ever more just to roam.

I had twelve ships to begin
We sacked another city and then
The people we sacked
Went and done got us back
And we were to sea once again.

We had attacked the Cicones.
When we left there were only low moans.
Took their twisted horn cattle
Cause they lost the battle
"Let's head for less dangerous zones.

Let's run the ships. Hey, let's go!"
But my men got drunk and said "No,
We have enough time
And captives and wine
We don't have to hurry no mo."

But the Cicones who had run away
Came back and they came to stay
With some of their friends
And the untimely ends
Of my sailors were timely that day.

Some of us made it back to the ships.
On board I offered some tips.
"To avoid you own killing
Try not to keep chillin'

Until the enemy comes back with his whips

Driving his damn armored division
Over you cause you made the decision
To not listen to me.
That is the key.
Men, this is your mission.

Now get your sad asses on board."
Then we embarked and a libation poured
And prayers quietly said
For all of our dead
Then the winds howled and screamed and roared.

Darkness then fell through the air.
Day after day we didn't know where
The hell we might be
And the reason, you see,
Is that *here* never was more than *there.*

Then at last the weather did clear
And we saw an island quite near.
How far did we go?
Man, that looks like snow!
And we didn't have no cold weather gear.

"Anybody know where our boat is?"
Somebody shouted "The Land of the Lotus!"
It was Heinrich Schliemann
A common seaman
Who was always blabbing about Herodotus.

Then it began to rain.
The weather seemed quite insane.
I was transfixed
Rain and snow mixed?
"The snow is powdered cocaine!"

Said Seaman Schliemann taking a breath

"And the rain is pure crystal meth
And the surrounding sea
Is sweet LSD
And the name of the city is Death!

Sail away! Sail away! O, my Captain!"
But I didn't know just what was happenin'
We seemed already on land
And you understand
I just smiled, said " Hey, what's happenin?"

Then I felt really quite mellow.
Saw a Lotus Eater. He seemed a fine fellow
I had a strange need
And smoked some fine weed.
Pretty soon we we're singing "Mellow Yellow!"

It seemed like a great place to stay.
What's up with going away?
And anyhow
I was Being There Now
Sitting on the dock of the bay!

I saw my men right there on the sand
Listening to some damn fine band
I think they said
It was "The Grateful Dead"
A name I can't understand.

I see it through some purple haze:
Schliemann is next to me, prays…
Then the Unmoved Mover
Sends the god J. Edgar Hoover
Who deplores our dope taking ways.

Next thing we know we're at Guantanamo
Which is a place you don't wanna go
We get waterboarded
And then are escorted

To the place called "Next Thing You Know!"

Next thing I knew we were at sea.
I thought "Man, what happened to me?
I was styling
Now I'm at Skull Island
Near the Isle of Innisfree!"

Now, don't you go and get me wrong
I got nothing against poor old King Kong
And I'll take Faye Ray
Almost any day
That is if Kong ain't along.

But we were on the Cyclopes side
Where wheat and barley and rich grape abide
But where a simple stranger
Is in mortal danger
Cause that's where the Cyclopes hide.

They are giant one-eyed hillbillies
Living up in them hillies
Hairy and gross
They are almost
Enough to give Achilles the willies.

The clouds were hiding the moon
And we sang a nautical tune
About a mystic isle
Where we'd abide awhile
And then get outta there soon.

We had to land. We were damn famished.
Our food had suddenly vanished
All we had…damn!
We're a few cans of Spam
Which was all the government could manage.

So we sailed in and then beached our boats

And were suddenly surrounded by goats.
So we dined on goat meat
Goat horns and goat feet
And from the skins made some goat coats.

We feasted. Man, how we styled.
We had flagons of Laffite Rothschild
We sat on the sand
A merry old band
And what happened next was wild.

Came Dawn, all of us were still drinking
And somebody got to thinking
"You know those One Eyes?
Maybe they're cool guys."
So we walked form the beach drunk and singing.

I made sure to take some mo wine.
Felt it would probably be fine:
"We'll just say Hello
Look around some and go
And the gods will give us a sign!"

We saw a big cave covered with ivy-o
With little sheep and sweet lambs a divie-o
And Marcy Dotes
And Maizy Oats
Though, on the whole quite jivie-o.

There was a great stone for a door
And all the sleepy sheep grazed right before
So we went right in
Swilling Coq de Vin
And layed around on the floor.

Layed around on the floor eating cheese
In a pleasantly warm summer breeze
My men said, "Let go."
But I replied "No."

Done in by the Drunkard's disease.

I said, "Man, I want see this!"
And gobbled some more cheese whiz.
When suddenly there loomed
The doomlist doomed
Crazy giant that there ever is.

He was at least sixty feet tall
Had one eye and just one ball.
And a succession
Of malevolent expressions
That I found, over all, very dull.

I felt, can I say, disappointed.
Here I was -- a fellow anointed
By the gods for a Fate
Designed to be great.
I felt like saying "Aroint it!

This is the best you can do?
Can't I meet a Famous Monster or two?
Can't I even aspire
To meet a vampire
Or a werewolf with a didgeridoo?

Those fellows are, at least, intellectual
Though, spiritually somewhat objectionable
But at least one could chat
And feel, somewhat, that
There's a higher meaning somewhat contextual.

I mean one senses a sign or a symbol
And one is not repelled by the pimple
On the monster's dumb face
When there is a curious grace
And not everything's so damn simple."

Here Odysseus was interrupted in his tale.

By Ahab who said "I know a white whale
Who is both symbol and sign
Of the demonic divine
Perhaps, you would like to sail..."

But Ahab never got to finish.
"Overall I felt quite diminished
By that old reliant
The One-Eyed Giant..."
And old Ahab knew he was finished.

"As I was saying it all felt very jejune-o
Give me a vampire and a scary old moon-o
And a spooky castle
And a passle
Of Abbeys gloomy and ruined-o.

So, Polyphemus (That's what he was called).
Seized two men, dashed their brains out and bawled
About how he don't care about Zeus
And uttered other obtuse
Remarks -- banal and quite dull.

He asks me "Hey, where are your ships?
And me --I'm good at these quips
Said, "We were washed ashore
Why'd you do that for?"
As he raised Demetrious to his lips.

I keep doing all that I can!
I tell him my name is No-Man!
He grabs two more Greeks
To stuff in his cheeks
And I come up with a plan.

Sadly we just can't elude
This monster so crass and rude
He rolls a great stone
As he sucks on a bone

And closes the entrance. We're screwed.

So I say, "Hey, do want some fine wine?"
And gave him all of mine
And with a little persuasion
And-re-orientation
Soon he's done on the floor and lying.

So then we had to work quick
And we got a great big old stick
Sharpened the end
So it would tend
To do what we wanted and quick.

So as soon as the monster is out
I stick the stick in the eye of that lout
Until he was blinded
And then I reminded
My crew what it all was about.

And did so as we ran from that fool
"My name is No-Man" I said quite cool
So when the other Cyclops
Came down from the treetops
Everything followed this rule.

"Oh, is some man hurting you, friend?"
"No man is hurting me!" The end.
So they all go away.
Shout "Have a nice day!"
Thinking "Polyphemus is just drinkin' again."

Book Ten
Aeolus, the Laestrygonians, and Circe

[Aeolia, Melancholia, Echolia]

Next we landed in Aeolia:
Which induced a certain melancholia
When your only solace
Is a guy like Aeolus
It also induces Echolia.

Is that me or is that just the wind?
You look around and you fell chagrined:
You ain't nothin' but dust
But you know that you must
Keep on going to the bitter bitter end.

Aeolus has six stalwart sons.
And guess what he's gone and done:
Married off each to a sister
Each Mrs. and Mr.
Told them to go and have fun.

There on that isle it seems a tenet
That no one is thought tormented
A windy old cluster
Of blustering blusterers
Just like the United States Senate.

So the bros marry the sisses
And nobody ever disses:
They're too busy blabbing
And too busy grabbin'
A variety of succulent dishes.

Their mouths full, they stand up to debate
In rhetoric baroque and ornate
Whether it's been as cool
As some other old fool
Asserts it has been of late.

Of course, I'm never at a loss

I grinned and called Aeolus the Boss
Told him where I'd been
Said I hoped to inherit the wind
Hoped that he's help us all get across.

So he gave me a bag full of breezes
For he was the Jesus of Breezes
Said, "Now you know
You can control where you go!"
Which seemed an excellent thesis.

So he summoned the wind from the west
To blow us home so ending our quest
And I gripped the sail rope
So full of hope
But, of course, this was only a test.

We sailed on for nine days and nights
Then saw the most lovely of sights
My own island home
No more would I roam.
And I'd soon be asserting my rights.

I was awake that whole damn time
But fell asleep in my own home clime
And my idiot crew…
What did they do
Again, committed a crime.

They said "Look what the old Captain's holdin'
I bet it's filled with things silver and golden!"
But it was the bag of the winds
And now it begins
Disaster -- just like I told them.

Seaman Schliemann replied with disdain
"It's probably full of powdered cocaine."
So they opened the sack
And it's a natural fact

Heigh-ho the wind and the rain.

The winds howled a scathing attack,
Swept us to Aeolia back
I covered my ass
Thought "This too shall pass!"
Sang "It's All For Me Grog and Tabac!"..:

Went and told Aeolus how we sinned
Asked him if he could help us again
"Hell, no. The end.
The answer my friend,
The answer is blowing in the wind."

Looked like we had to go.
The answer was a big NOOOOOOOOOO..
So we set out to sea
Poor, poor pitiful me.
Heigh ho the carrion crow.

For seven days and nights we all rowed
Till we came to the evil abode
Of Gigantiswhipassess
Lords of the passes
To reap just what we had sowed.

There were giants on the earth in those days
Beware of their sick evil ways:
Those Laestrygonians
Are pandemonium.
Those weren't the good old days.

All but my ship pulled into the bay
I steered my stout ship a little away
And climbed up a cliff
To try to see if
There was some place we could stay.

I had sent three men on before

Saying "Tell them were from the Trojan war.
And blessed by Zeus
And we come bearing news...
Just try to establish rapport."

There they were now running back!
Screaming that we were attacked.
I found out anon
That one man was gone
Antiphates had turned him into a snack.

And there just over the bay
A few giants coming our way
My own black ship
Might give them the slip
But...oh my poor men…no way!

And I watched as the giants devoured them
While spewing forth vile apothegms.
And we, cunning dastards,
Rowed like whipped bastards
There was no way we were going to follow them.

Farewell my companions! We'll see ya!
We're rowing to the isle of Aeaea
We felt quite sad
Yet quite relieved. Quite glad.
As I broke out the sailor's panacea.

There were sixty bottles of rum
And we dutifully drank every one
Thanking fate with kind words
That we weren't to be turds
Emerging from some giant's bung."

By then it was 2 AM.
O was thinking of himself -- not thinking of them.
He looked about.

They all had passed out
Except for Ahab who was saying "Ahem...

Thar she blows! A hump like a snow-hill!"
(This gave Odysseus a cheap thrill).
Then Ahab did beg
"Pull my wooden leg
Oh, whale! thou glidest on! Kill! Kill! Kill!"

Perhaps, it's a tender mercy.
Odysseus forgot all about Circe.
If you really care
It's all still there
In The Odyssey, "Curse ye!

Furl the top gallant-sails, oh
And close the reef top sails, oh
Break out the main hold
Are ye harpooners bold?
Up! Keep a good eye upon the whale. oh!"

With that old Ahab crumbled.
And Odysseus felt somewhat humbled
By a mad man true
Red, white, and blue.
Outside the thunder did rumble.

Queequeg woke up: "Um Um Um
Plenty too much thunder. Not enough rum!"
Then like a mad fiend
He beat his green tambourine.
"We don't want thunder; we want rum!"

Ah, there seemed no reason nor rhyme
Odysseus bolted back his gin and lime
And the barkeep
Who had been asleep
Said, "Hurry up, please. It's time!"

Book Eleven
Odysseus Meets the Shades of the Dead

[Henry James, To Hell and Back]

Odysseus didn't dig his lingo
And was thinking of the Distinguished Thing-o.
Started to play.
What could he say?
All he could do was sing-o.

Odysseus

"I'm just as guy with a banjo
And I ain't doing too well
But what you got to understand, oh
Is that I recently came back from Hell.

And there I saw my old mother
And many of my so long lost pals
Yes, I'm drinking and I'll have another
Ah, these dear guys and gals

Tirisias
"Oh, Jesus what are you doing here?"

Odysseus
"I wanta go home. I'm all alone."

Tiresias

 I wish I could buy a beer."

Odyseus

I think I'll never see my old home

Sometimes it seems just so hard
Like I'm stuck in a damn epic poem
By a bullockbefriending bard."

Teresias

You will lose all your companions
But at least find your weary way home
And linger under the banyans
And have your own designer cologne!

Odysseus

I saw poor old Achilles
And here's what the poor boy said
"Being here gives you the willies
Nobody is better off dead

I'd give all my fame and my glory
And be a sad ghost with no name
If I could be in another story
Just another guy out in the rain.

Sometimes I dream of Manhattan
The one that there never was
And nights of sadness and satin
And you know the reasons because

I'm made in the shade – got no reason
But eternal unreality
In Hell season after season
Poor, poor pitiful me."

Oh, you can call me Ishmael
Or you can call my Odysseus
All I can say. I ain't doing too well.
My name's Ernesto Bognino O'Sisyphus.

Now, I don't mean to alarm us

So, here's just what I'll do.
Put on my Ungrateful Dead pajamas
And learn to play the didgeridoo.

I'm just as guy with a banjo
And I ain't doing too well
But what you got to understand, oh
Is that I recently came back from Hell.

I'm just a poor man with a banjo
How can I find my wife and my son?
What I hope you understand, oh
One day everything's done."

Then they all awoke from their dreams
Into the world of "It Seems"
Judging by how much they drank
Their dreams were all blank.
A Love Supreme! A Love Supreme!

Then they all ordered some shawarma.
And Odysseus sang "Nessun Dorma."
Ahab looked out
Said, "With out any doubt
We're in for a goddamn big storm-a."

Guardi le stelle
Che tremano d'amore e di speranza...
Ma il mio mistero è chiuso in me,
Il nome mio nessun saprà!

Book Twelve
**The Sirens, Scylla and Charybdis, the Cattle of the
Sun**

**[The Crystal fretting of the Multiverse Impends, The
Thunderwords, Ahab keeps on keeping on, The**

141

Gong-Tormented Sea]

If you're like me, you've been wondering
What's up with this copious thundering.
Like young Alice said:
Go feed your head.
You know there must have been nearly a hundred

Cracks in the crystal fretting.
You won't lose if you're betting.
And if you're in the habit
Of following the white rabbit
You know there is no forgetting

Not really of the warp and the woof.
There's no holding yourself aloof:
You open the latch
And there's a bandersnatch
And things as they are go poof.

Datta. Dayadhvam. Damyata.
Or just in case you kinda forgot a
contransmagnificandjewbangtantiality
Of an alternate reality
A kind of extended fermata.

They all felt the lonely absurds
As they heard these thunderwords
Ahab looked out
Then shouted out
"Words! Words! Words!

bababadalgharaghtakamminarronnkonnbronntonnerronnt
uonnthunntrovarrhounawnskawntoohoohoordenenthurnu

Perkodhuskurunbarggruauyagokgorlayorgromgremmitgh
undhurthrumathunaradidillifaititillibumullunukkunun

klikkaklakkaklaskaklopatzklatschabattacreppycrottygrad
daghsemmihsammihnouithappluddyappladdypkonpkot

Bladyughfoulmoecklenburgwhurawhorascortastrumpapo
rnanennykocksapastippatappatupperstrippuckputtanach

Thingcrooklyexineverypasturesixdixlikencehimaroundhe
rsthemaggerbykinkinkankanwithdownmindlookingated

Lukkedoerendunandurraskewdylooshoofermoyportertoor
yzooysphalnabortansporthaokansakroidverjkapakkapuk

Bothallchoractorschumminaroundgansumuminarumdrum
strumtruminahumptadumpwaultopoofoolooderamaunstur
nup

Pappappapparrassannuaragheallachnatullaghmonganmac
macmacwhackfalltherdebblenonthedubblandaddydoodle

husstenhasstencaffincoffintussemtossemdamandamnacos
aghcusaghhobixhatouxpeswchbechoscashlcarcarcaract

Ullhodturdenweirmudgaardgringnirurdrmolnirfenrirlukki
lokkibaugimandodrrerinsurtkrinmgernrackinarockar

And I thought I saw Leopold Bloom
There in an upper room
Of the Spouter Inn
With Finnegan.
Or how can I presume?

And Ahab leads each able man
To Rick's fabled Café Américain
Always seafaring
The awful daring
And besides he really liked Sam.

Ahab said, "Ok, play it again."

Odysseus said, "I remember when
I was in a poem
And couldn't get home
We sailed back to Circe and then

She gave us some sort of advice.
"Don't look back. Don't think twice.
And remember what Byron
Said about the Sirens
Nothing else will ever suffice

But to put wax in your sailor's ears
As near the sirens they steer.
But if you want to hear them,
As you draw near them
Take all that nautical gear

The ropes and the chains and the padlocks
And fasten them to the oarlocks
And before the mast
Make yourself fast
You got all of that, Sherlock?

And then, perhaps, you can listen
As they sing of that one and this one
In immortal love
Sent from above
And how their dear bones glisten

In a cave beneath the sea
They are calling, they are calling to thee
And your sweet wife is drowned
And all around
Is strange beauty of the highest degree.

It will be the Deep Blue Goodbye
You'll want to live there and so you will die
Any pleasure you took...
The Long Lavender Look..."

She looked sweetly at me. Did sigh.

So ho! for the Empty Copper Sea.
My stout crewmen and me.
A Tan and Sandy Silence
Without ideals, without violence
And, oh! The difference to me.

We sailed through The Lonely Silver Rain
Rain then sun again
One Fearful Yellow Eye
In the Dreadful Lemon Sky
Then again The Lonely Silver Rain.

The wind was a Turquoise Lament
Darker Than Amber the evenings that sent
The meteor's Free Fall in Crimson
And the inexpressible frisson
Of leaning against the mast and smoking a Kent.

We sailed into the Horse Latitudes
As I strove to correct their attitudes
A knowing ennui
Is just the thing for the sea
And a knowledge of the sailor's beatitudes.

But my men lacked the bel esprit
For which I had the master's degree
They brought out the rope
But I had little hope
"I do not think they will sing to me."

But they sang to me like no other
And they sang to me of my dear brother
Travis McGee
On the wine-dark sea
But I'm Odysseus, so why did they bother?

"Come," they sang, "It's not far

To slip F-18 at Bahia Mar
And that's not all
Chookie McCall
Waits for thee at the built-in bar.

And Meyer is on the John Maynard Keynes
See how sweetly he leans
With the lovelychildren
And Puss Gillian
Nobody knows what it means.

Hear the seas sounds, the rush
Of the waters past the Busted Flush
In Time and In Space
A new and wonderful case
And the melancholy, expected hush

Of all beauty when you then arise!
What strange stars and strange skies
As the plot begins
With Boodles gin
And a solo by Sonny Rollins dies!"

I cried out. But I was ignored
They had wax in their ears heretofore.
I wanted to be
Travis McGee
And Odyssey here no more no more!

But we rowed past -- all the lovely songs
As the Sirens shimmied in sexy sarongs
I was released
Then it was on to the beast.
The sea was tormented by gongs.

Oh, the gong-tormented sea
Dolphin torn and snot green though it be
Whatever that means
Makes for wonderful scenes

And double damn fine poetry.

I had forgotten to tell my men
That it looked like six of them
We're gonna be dead
That's what Circe said
But I was only looking out for them.

For Charybdis it seemed quite certain
Would mean, for all of us, curtains
If we chose Scylla
That beastly Godzilla
Only six would be hurtin'

Because she had six hungry heads,
And never ever took none of her meds.
And eighteen sets of teeth,
And foul breath that seethed
With the decaying flesh of the dead.

So we went and rowed on past her
"Boys, I said, You better row faster."
But it was no use
She sank each ugly tooth
Into the hides of six poor sad bastards.

When she took them they cried out to me!
But that's death on the Dark Copper Sea.
And so we wept
Drank and then slept
And came to Thrinacia by 3."

Of, course, Odysseus continued his story
But Homer got it all down before he
Got to this part.
The fellow lacked art.
So we won't get into it anymore he

Had as early as the first damn book

Told how the poor sailors cooked
The Oxen of the Sun
And when they were done
Were wriggling on Poseidon's hook.

And all about Odysseus and Calypso.
He did it facto ipso
So we will conclude
This strange interlude
And take a few lingering nips-oh

Of Boodles the Gin that's preferred
By Travis McGee. Have you heard.
John MacDonald is dead
That's what they said.
And I find it all very absurd.

Books Thirteen through Twenty-Four

['Hark! 'tis an elfin-storm from faery land,
  "Of haggard seeming, but a boon indeed:
  "Arise—arise! the morning is at hand;—]

Odysseus looked up. It was day.
The free French sang La Marseilles
Sam was asleep
And dark dreams did keep
Rick awake all night in his café.

Outside the warp and woof trembled
Overall you might say it resembled
What's going on
In the Gospel of John
And beings sentient and nonsentient assembled

In the sky above the Time and Space Port

Where possibilities of every sort
Reclaim transcendence
In a way that's quite splendid
Revoking the claims of La Morte.

"Away!," Ahab cried "The Pequod
Waits for us -- nor other men nor gods
I'll continue my quest
But I think it is best
For you to go home. Damn it's odd.

And I think it's worth asking just why
You will live and I'll have to die
Because I rage against IS
The Nothingness Biz
While you long for your dear wife and sigh

And you are considered the wanderer
Though exposed as a poor blunderer
While my mission
Ends in Nuclear fission!"
Thundered Ahab the Asunderer.

And the Band played "The Leaving of Liverpool"
And Odysseus played "The Flop Eared Mule"
And there was Grace
All over the place
Which is something you won't learn in school.

Odysseus went aboard, fell asleep
And the Pequod made it over the deep
And he still was snoozing
As they went cruising
Ahab said, "I have promises to keep."

Odysseus snoozed. They made land!
Ahab left them there on the strand
Beneath the Steel Pier
And he thought it quite queer

To awake to a Dixieland band.

And there in the air -- A Flying Horse!
It wasn't Pegasus, of course
But a horse named José
Owned by Dennis O'Day
Who jumped with negligent force

From a Diving Platform right there
Then plunging through the salt air
Into a pool.
Nothing so cool
Come to Ithaca since before the la Guerre.

Now the plot is beginning to thicken
On the boardwalk there is a chicken
That, well, you know,
Can play Tic Tac Toe.
On a bench Mr. Pickwick from Dickens

Looks out at the glowing salt sea
And who's passing by? Hey, it's me!
With my dear old Dad
And I feel rather sad
So I pleaded with Dad so that he

Would get me some saltwater taffy
And a number of comics about Daffy
That strange goddamn Duck
But I'm having no luck.
For my father's had too much black cafee.

And it's father and son on a quest
My father thinks it is best
At this late date
To micturate
At our hotel, then rest

In our rooms on Baltic Avenue
Yes, right there. What can you do?
If you are the son
Of a son of a gun
Who's had too much café? You're through.

But you saw the old diving horse
And the Monster of the Sea, of course
Will be on display
For just one more day
And your Dad with irresistible force

Is dragging you through '58
And, seeing that now I say."Wait!"
All that is gone
Keeps going on
The white rabbit tells you, "You're late!"

Ah, you still don't get the idea?
Well, Odysseus now begins his career.
But Vaudeville is dead
So George Burns said
"We better get outta here."

And Odysseus says "Where's my son?"
And Telemachus came on the run
And then who did they see
But Penelope
Singing "Ain't We Got Fun."

They glide, they glide like ghosts
Past all readers with their broken remotes.
Yes, they fled away
Just on that day.
They're gone. Didn't leave any notes.

Finis

HAVLINS
25¢ MATINEES
EVERY · DAY ·
GALLERY 10¢
HAVLIN'S
THEATRE
HAVLIN'S
THE

When Omer smote is bloomin lyre;
He'd eard men speak by land and sea;
And what he thought e might require
E went and took --the same as me!